Fill up to Spill out

Because we can't pour from an empty cup

Allison R. Smith

Copyright © 2020 Allison R. Smith

All rights reserved.

ISBN: 9798561667589

Dedication

For my husband Ted
and our beautiful girls, Avery and Natalie.
Thank you for filling my cup each day.

Table of Contents

INTRODUCTION	1
FILL UP WITH SELF-CARE	11
FILL UP WITH ORDER & SIMPLICITY	29
FILL UP WITH COMMUNITY	43
FILL UP WITH FUN	53
FILL UP WITH REST	61
FILL UP WITH PERSONAL GROWTH	69
FILL UP WITH COURAGE	79
FILL UP WITH GOALS	89
FILL UP WITH WISE CHOICES	99
FILL UP BY ENCOURAGING OTHERS WITH YOUR GIFTS	109
FILL UP WITH JESUS	119
CONCLUSION	129

Introduction

How do we truly become the very best version of ourselves? That's the big question I have been trying to answer over the last several years as everyone in the personal growth space seems to be telling us to "become the best version of yourself" and "live your best life." I'm a huge fan of personal growth, and I'm all about living my best life, but what is it that we are trying to achieve? What does our very best self really look like? What is it that we need to be chasing? What goal do we need to achieve in order to feel like we are living our best life? Is it the dream job with a generous six-figure salary? The beautiful house with the white picket fence? The perfect marriage with 2.5 kids and a well-trained dog? The ideal body with six-pack abs and long beautiful lashes? A successful business? A New York Times Bestseller? 10,000 followers so we can get the swipe-up? A life filled with traveling and fun adventures? All the latest greatest things? Hustle-filled days full of personal accomplishments and happiness for achieving them?

My friends like to use the phrase "living the dream" or LTD for short. I think we all heard that quote for the first time in the 2005 hit-comedy, Wedding Crashers. If you've seen the movie, then you remember that famous scene with Will Ferrell and Owen Wilson when Will's character says, "I'm just living the dream." I hear that phrase all the time now, but what does LTD really mean? Is it just a catchy line we like to use to label one of those truly awesome days or experiences, or does it mean that we have finally achieved what feels like our very best life (hopefully not crashing weddings and living with Mom and her meatloaf)?

As we strive to become this best version of ourselves and live our best lives, are we transforming ourselves into who we or others think we should be, or are we fully embracing who God *made* us to be? What is it that produces happiness and true fulfillment in life? A life full of success or a life filled with peace, joy, and purpose no matter the circumstances?

I've been on this pursuit of becoming a better version of myself for probably the last decade, and it's in the last few years that I have really defined what I think it means to be my best self and live my best life. The best version of myself embraces who I am and who I am becoming as a follower of Christ. It looks like taking care of myself so I can be my best self. It looks like taking time to fill my cup each day so that I have an abundance of energy to love and serve others. Living my best life or living the dream is pursuing a life filled with peace, joy, and purpose each day. It's focusing on what truly matters and saying no to the things that don't. It's finding the good in every season and situation. It's not living life for me but living life to serve and encourage others. It's creating greatness even when life isn't so great.

I wish that life could always be great. It's pretty easy to feel like we are living the dream or living our best life when everything is going well, right? But if you've been living long enough you know that life can be pretty tough sometimes. Our journey through life is often filled with painful bumps in the road, long detours, and empty tanks. Things happen, our plans change, and certain seasons are just downright busy, exhausting, sad, and disappointing. It's not always easy to find peace and joy or the good in a situation when we feel like we are simply surviving and definitely not thriving.

The important question we need to ask is, can we still pursue the best version of ourselves and live our best lives when life is not so great? Is there still a way to fill our cup in order to create energy when we simply feel depleted? Can we find purpose in our most challenging seasons? Is there a way to cultivate peace in the chaos and joy through our sadness? Are we able to find the good in situations that don't feel so good?

These are all great questions, and I think the answer is, although we can't control a lot of what happens each day, we still have a choice in the way we show up for ourselves and others. *Choose* is such a powerful word, and sometimes we forget that despite what's going on around us, we still get to choose our mood, our attitude, and our actions. We choose our perspective and mindset. We choose what we consume, create, and share. Life is not always going to be great, but yes, we can still create greatness.

I was feeling pretty great as I embarked on this journey of writing a second book, hoping to inspire and encourage people in a more tactical way. I had just published my first book sharing my own story and personal transformation journey, giving me a new-found sense of courage and confidence like never before. I was feeling ambitious and energetic about the best version of myself that I was pursuing. I had learned to create joy and purpose in my own life and wanted to use my words to encourage others to do the same.

2020 was off to a great start, filled with reflection over the last decade and anticipation and fired-up excitement about a new decade and year ahead. I had big dreams and goals, a full calendar, and a plan with such clarity it probably sounded crazy to those who knew about it. Growth had been my theme over the last 10 years as my husband and I grew our family, careers, and our home while courage and impact were the two words I was focusing on for this next decade in my 40's.

I was organized and ready for what would be a busy, but memorable year for our family. My eagerness led me to filling out all the calendars and planners with our schedules, activities, important events, and goals. My girls and I even made vision boards for the first time ever. We had big plans for travel and fun adventures, celebrations and weddings in 2020. Our girls had just gotten their first passports, and we looked forward to our first international trip together to visit our military family in Germany. We booked an awesome house for our 11th annual beach trip with our friends, and we were also looking forward to a trip to Mexico to celebrate a college friend's 40th birthday. Our summer was going to be amazing.

In early February I completed my 3rd full marathon in celebration of turning 40 the previous month. I had simultaneously trained for the race while writing my first book, my two ambitious goals for turning 40. Go big or go home, right? We took family photos that very same day (because I am crazy, and our original date got rained out) to promote my book and new blog and to celebrate life and all our many blessings. With sore legs but a very full heart, I smiled and laughed while our photographer captured some great shots of our family. Our dog even took a swim in the pond of our college campus, ending our family photo session with a bang. It was a really good LTD kind of day.

And as if that wasn't enough excitement for the year, a few weeks later, my husband successfully defended his dissertation for his doctorate degree in education at Baylor University. After six long years of hard work and sacrifice, determination and persistence (and many tears from his mostly supportive wife), it was finally his day to shine. He did it, and we were so proud and couldn't wait to see him walk across the stage a few months later for his hooding ceremony and much deserved diploma. So many things were going right in our world, and the year was just getting started. 2020 was on target to be a stellar year for our family. And maybe you were feeling that way too. Like us, you had big plans and expectations, goals and aspirations. It was a new year, a new decade, and it just felt like it was going to be great. But 2020 was only great until it wasn't great anymore. It would definitely be a memorable year, but for very different reasons.

That's the crazy thing about life. It's wildly unpredictable and most definitely not fair. Everything can be going great until something changes in a flash. And that's what happened in March of 2020 in a big way for literally everyone on this planet. We were already shocked and saddened by the tragic death of Kobe Bryant, his daughter and friends in late January, but no one could have predicted what else was coming our way. Life as we knew it literally came to a screeching halt as spring break ended for a lot of the kids in our country. All of our routines and plans were completely disrupted as the entire world was suddenly flipped upside down, or at least it felt that way. Spring break was instantly the longest spring break in history.

    I had just begun writing this book when everything changed. I knew I wanted to write a book in 2020 encouraging others with this idea of filling up to spill out in order to be the best version of themselves, but I had no idea what kind of season I would be writing it in. I started this book in February when life was pretty great. I felt like I was in a good position to encourage others, specifically busy moms like me, to make time for themselves, learning how to fill their cup in order to cultivate peace, joy, and purpose in their life. So, when life suddenly got crazy, I was naturally tempted to put this project on hold. After all, why would anyone want to read about living your best life or filling your cup in a season of change and hardship, a season when most people were just trying to survive. It suddenly felt hard.

    I too was struggling with the confusing change and uncertainty all around me. Like everyone else, my family and I were just trying to navigate our way through a season we had not planned for. I was disappointed and sad about everything I was having to draw a line through on my calendar. I was frustrated with the changes at my work and our kids not getting to go to school and finish out the year. I felt a little bitter about my husband getting to work from home with our girls, while I was considered essential and had to report to work every day wearing a mask.

    I stopped writing for several weeks, not sure if the timing was right for this book or if it would ever be right, but then I decided to come back to it. I came to the realization that God put this particular book on my heart in 2020, because He wanted me to write it when life wasn't so great. He wanted me to find a way to cultivate peace, joy, and purpose in real-time as I wrote this book about filling your cup. Writing wasn't just for my readers but was also for me in a stressful season when I needed it. Writing gave me a much-needed creative and therapeutic outlet to really process what I was going through during a tough season. I needed something else to focus on besides my healthcare job which was stressful. I needed a distraction from all the negativity in the news and on social media. I needed to learn how to keep filling my own cup in a season filled with disappointment. God was calling me to intentionally focus on what truly mattered and to encourage others to do the same.

So, here we are. As I continue to write this book during the year of 2020, we are living through Coronavirus (Covid-19), and life is strangely different and challenging and most certainly frustrating. We are making history as each week and month passes by. We are being told to stay home, wash our hands (because apparently, we weren't washing them before), practice social distancing, home-school our children (also known as virtual learning), and do everything we can to slow down the spread of this novel virus. Flatten the curve is what they are urging us to do, but it's more like flatten our tires, as we feel stranded from the life we were comfortable with and loved. We were made for community, to do life with others, to go places and do things, and we are now being told to just be still.

It's become strangely difficult to find things like toilet paper, cleaning products, and grocery items. The media has caused people to panic-buy and hoard. Big box stores are literally wiped out clean, while small businesses have been forced to close their doors. It doesn't seem fair. We are inconvenienced, saddened, and fearful for what lies ahead. Every event, activity, and gathering of people has been marked off our calendar. School is closed for the remainder of the school year, and it's unclear when or how kids will return to the classroom. Colleges look like ghost towns. The much-anticipated summer Olympics have even been cancelled. And sadly, lots of weddings are being postponed or changed to much smaller intimate gatherings.

Everyone is having to adapt to this new Covid way of life. People are shopping for essential items while wearing a mask or any sort of face covering and standing 6 feet away from others. Plexi glass and floor stickers telling us where to stand has become part of the new and interesting shopping experience. Essential workers are on the frontlines, learning to provide goods and services in new and creative ways. More people are turning to online shopping or curbside pickup than ever before. Everything seems to be going virtual including school, meetings, and doctor's visits. Some healthcare workers are working harder than ever before wearing the same mask for more days than they'd like to count, and others are being sent home as elective procedures and non-urgent care is being put on hold. Millions of people are losing their jobs, including healthcare workers in the middle of a healthcare crisis which seems absolutely crazy. Gas prices are dropping. What's considered essential versus non-essential is confusing as liquor stores are left open, while our churches and hair salons have been forced to close their doors.

We are spending much more time in our homes than ever before. It's become political, media-driven, and divisive, and it doesn't seem to be going away. Covid-19 is being called a global pandemic, but what it feels like is a really bad dream. Except that we are not waking up from this nightmare. We feel trapped, isolated, and overwhelmed by the change. It's turning into an economic crisis like no other, and there is literally no end in sight. It's hard to know what to believe or who to believe anymore, as everything feels so terribly wrong.

As we're learning and adapting to this new "normal," we miss the life we knew filled with friends, school, activities and job security. Filling our cup suddenly feels like an impossible task when our rhythms and routines have been completely disrupted. If it's not the virus itself, it's the closure of the country and all the social distancing that's made life feel so hard. It's tempting to just want to throw in the towel, "let everything go," and just simply survive this crazy season we've been dealt. Why should we care about investing in ourselves and living our best lives in a year filled with hardship? Why should I even keep writing this book? Or running when all my races have been cancelled? Why does anything really matter right now?

Well, it matters because life goes on, and like everything else, this too shall pass (or at least we hope it does). It's possible to reframe this time and this season as a gift and not the curse that it feels like right now. We were not made to just go through life, but bravely grow through life and all it's difficult seasons. This is our time to learn and grow and encourage others while doing so. It's important to fill our cups each day so we can be strong for those who need us. Just like our car can only go so far on empty, we too must stop and refuel to keep going. If we want to continue to live a life filled with peace, joy, and purpose, we must learn to fill our cup even when times are hard.

Especially when times are hard.

Now is the perfect time to focus on what truly matters.

If we want to create energy and a feeling of inner peace and joy no matter the circumstances, we must take care of ourselves in a way that produces it. We must make time to fill up in order to spill out to others, hence the title of this book and my blog, "Fill up to Spill out, because we can't pour from an empty cup."

But what should we be pouring into our cup each day? What is it that refuels us when our tank is running dry? What gives us the energy we need to do the things we wish to do? When I tell you to fill your cup, what is it that comes to mind?

Do you think of coffee or tea?

Hot or iced?

Starbuck's or Dunkin' Donuts?

Well, if you're paying, I'll take a holiday cup filled with a non-fat dirty chai latte please. Or maybe just a coffee with my favorite seasonal pumpkin spice creamer (don't you think it should be available year-round?). Coffee is the fuel we need to keep going. Coffee is the answer to all of life's problems, and coffee fixes everything (or wine if it's after 5).

I'm joking, but that does sound delicious, right? We all love our coffee and our wine, or some version of liquid deliciousness in our lives. But what I am talking about is so much more than your morning cup of joe or evening glass of wine, although I rarely start or end my day without one.

The fuel I'm referring to is a much larger investment in what truly matters. It's intentionally pursuing the things that give us energy and bring us peace, joy, and purpose every single day. It's spending time doing the things that fill us up and allow us to function at our very best. This time we invest in ourselves and the things that truly matter is time well spent. In fact, it's an essential component to living a life of purpose, impact, and service to others. We cannot serve well or love well if we are not pouring

Fill up to Spill out

back into ourselves. If we are not taking care of our own health, learning and growing, resting and refueling, we don't perform well. We don't love well, lead well, or take care of things well.

I know this from personal experience and also because of my job as a health care provider. I'm a working mom with a day job as a family nurse practitioner in a community clinic. I see lots of busy moms like me (and dads too) that are not pouring into themselves. They do *all* the things for *all* the people without ever taking time to fill their own cup. They are tired and drained and say they never have time for themselves. They are literally running on empty.

They often come to me feeling anxious, depressed, overwhelmed, exhausted, unhealthy, and unfulfilled. They want to feel better, have more energy, feel calmer and less anxious, and they are often looking for an easy fix, a pill or supplement or something to "fill them up."

A lot of them do leave with a pill for their mood or to help them sleep (and there's nothing wrong with that), but what they really need to do is make time for themselves. They need to exercise, eat healthy, go to therapy, listen to podcasts, read their Bible, organize their life, set goals for themselves, find ways to cultivate the peace and joy they desire, and ask for help. They need to work on filling their own cup so they can be the better spouse, parent, worker, and friend they wish to be.

When I am not pouring into my own physical, mental, and spiritual health every single day, I have much less to give to others. When I am not creating pockets of time in my day to fill my cup and protect my peace, I do not feel my best, and therefore the people around me do not receive my best. Instead, they get the depleted unhappy version of me, and who really wants that?

My people deserve a loving, present and patient, and encouraging wife, mom, daughter, friend, coworker, and healthcare provider. I need to be able to show up and be the best version of myself each and every day. I need to show up not only on the good days, but the tough ones too. I need to keep showing up even in the middle of this global pandemic.

In the following chapters, I will be sharing some of the things that have helped me fill my cup over the years as I pursue my very best life. My goal in writing this book is to encourage you through my own journey and personal experiences to cultivate peace, joy, and purpose in your life as well. Each chapter will include some of the ways I've learned to fill my cup in order to serve others as my very best self.

And as I'm writing this book during the middle of the 2020 Covid pandemic, I will also be sharing my personal experiences, perspective, and lessons learned in real-time as I walk through it. I will end the book with the chapter, filling up with Jesus, because without Him at the core of everything in my life, without my faith as the foundation, nothing really matters. Nothing fills us up like the one who gave His life for us. He fills our cup with love, joy, hope and peace. He restores us like no other, filling our cup in a way that naturally flows out to others. I hope you'll find this book to be helpful and encouraging, but most of all I hope you'll embrace who God made you to be, while pursuing who you are becoming through Him.

Chapter 1

Fill up with self-care

"Self-care is giving the world the best of you, instead of what's left of you." Katie Reed

I'm not sure if tween girls do this anymore, but when I was in junior high (many, many moons ago), we'd have something called "slumber parties" to celebrate all of our birthdays. Imagine 5-10 girls under one roof, watching movies, mixing cassette tapes on our pink boom box, eating popcorn and too much candy, giggling and giving each other make-overs late into the night. Sounds like a great time, right? Our parents would probably beg to differ as these parties would often bring big drama and little sleep, but us girls thought they were a blast. Make-up, manicures, apricot face masks, and crazy hair brought us so much joy (except for that time we went home with lice, ewe). Times were different back then. It wasn't about the way we looked or all the selfies we took and posted on social media throughout the night, but simply the laughter and the memories that were made on those special weekends. A simple sleepover in the 90's was all about time with our friends with a little pampering and fun. It was "self-care." We just didn't know anything about that yet.

In this new world of smart phones, selfies and social media, the term "self-care" can sometimes get sort of an eye-roll these days. Marketing as well as over-sharing has taken over our newsfeeds. Carefully cropped and filtered photos of people's feet soaking as they get a pedicure while sipping a latte or awkward selfies of women wearing face masks are the images that frequently come up if you search the hashtag "self-care." Go ahead and try it. Search #selfcare and see what pops up.

Why do we think people actually want to see our ugly feet? Or our bath water running? Or our face covered in a creamy white mask? These photos make me laugh. But I get it. Self-care is important, and sometimes it does look like getting our nails done or taking care of our skin or treating ourselves to a luxurious spa day with mimosas and friends (sign me up!). And because we are living in such a digital world, we often feel the need to post about it. We want to show people that we are taking time for ourselves.

But self-care is also so much more than pampering our feet, and what I find is that we tend to neglect the very basic things that could make us feel better on an everyday basis. We don't have to wait for a pedicure every 3 months to fill our cup. There's no need to wait for a night out with friends or a Sunday night to enjoy a hot bath, quickly to be disturbed by the kids wondering what we are doing.

Self-care is about so much more, and we should invest in it every single day. *Every* day? You ask. Yes, *every* day.

Self-care is loving yourself enough to take care of your physical, mental, and emotional needs *every* single day. It's filling your cup by not just being occasionally pampered and having that incredibly awkward selfie to prove it, but really investing in being your very best self. It's *real* things that make a big difference. It's self-love and respect, and it's not selfish at all. We can't give what we don't have. We can't love others if we don't love who God created us to be. We must love ourselves and take care of the body that God gave us in order to love others well. We must love who we are and who we are becoming as we journey through this one and only life.

"Love God, love others" is what we often hear, but I feel like our motto should be "Love God, take care of the person He made you to be, and then go love others well."

When we are not prioritizing self-care, we do not feel our best and therefore do not give our best. If you're anything like me, we have lots of people who depend on us, and we want to show up well for them. We want to have energy and an abundance of love to give. We want to be a good spouse, a good parent, a good worker, a good steward of our home and our finances, a good friend, and so much more. But if we aren't taking care of our own needs every day, how can we take care of the people and responsibilities around us?

Our lives are busier than ever before. Our calendars are full (except when something like coronavirus hits and wipes them clean). We have endless responsibilities including jobs, kids, a spouse, pets, a home and cars to maintain, bills, family, friends, church, cooking, shopping, laundry, and all sorts of endless tasks. And that's just when all the things are going smoothly without unexpected challenges that often arise. The mental load that moms often carry is exhausting. And some dads feel it too.

"Who has practice tonight, and who's getting them there?"

"Did I take out the meat to thaw before dinner?"

"Did I change out the laundry this morning?"

"Did I buy the gift for the birthday party on Saturday?"

"Did I mail back the RSVP in time?"

"Who has a spelling test to study for this week?"

"Did I wash the uniform for the game tomorrow?"

We can feel like we are running on a hamster wheel with no end in sight. And as we run on that wheel, like my daughter's hamster Patches likes to do late at night, it seems as if no one seems to notice. We just keep going and going and going. We do what has to be done. We just keep running. We just keep giving.

But we eventually find ourselves feeling empty. Our tank is drained. Our well is dry. Our cup needs to be filled up but with much more than just a latte.

When we put everyone and everything else above our own needs, we eventually lose ourselves. It becomes harder and harder to experience peace and joy. We just feel tired. Really, really tired.

Functioning at a self-less survival-mode kind of level eventually causes us to feel overwhelmed, exhausted, unfulfilled, unappreciated, resentful, and just like a car running on empty, we eventually break down if we don't fill up. Can you relate? We've all been there. We've had busy seasons in our life when we neglected areas of our own health, because we chose to prioritize the needs of everyone and everything else. We made work a priority. We chose our kids and all their needs and desires above our own. We chose to volunteer all our time and energy, leaving none for ourselves. We chose to show up for everyone else while not showing up for the person in the mirror. Maybe we felt like we didn't have a choice. We felt like self-care was selfish and that our work and kids were more important. We simply told ourselves that we just didn't have time to invest in ourselves.

But not having time is just another excuse we like to use. I get it, we're busy, but we all have time; we just use it differently. We choose to get that extra hour of sleep instead of waking up and using that time for ourselves. We choose to watch TV in the evening instead of going for run or reading a book to gain knowledge. We waste time scrolling through social media when we could be using that time to meal-prep, go for a walk, or be creative. We choose to numb out with something easy instead of choosing something healthy and wise. It's a choice, and not taking the time to care for our own health and the things that are essential to our well-being eventually results in burn-out. That light that has the ability to shine bright for God and for others simply goes out. It's like a gas-powered flame that runs out when the tank suddenly goes empty. That flame that burned bright before can't keep glowing without replacing the gas. We too need fuel to keep going.

We cannot care for those around us if we are not caring for ourselves. It's just like when we fly or go on a cruise and they tell

Fill up to Spill out

us to put our own oxygen mask or life vest on before assisting those around us. It's great advice, and we should take it. We can't be of help to someone else if we are struggling ourselves.

But if we take care of our own needs first, we give our best to those around us. And when we set a good example for others, it naturally spills out to those who are watching. It's all about giving others something great to imitate. When our kids see us investing in ourselves, they too see the importance of self-care. They too will make the time to pour into themselves, so they have more to give to the world.

So, what does this look like? What am I referring to when I tell you to invest in yourself? If self-care isn't just pedicures and lattes, then what is it?

Well, it might seem boring or elementary, but when I refer to self-care that truly fills you up, I am talking about basic but essential needs like taking a shower, washing your hair, eating regular nutritious meals, getting proper sleep, exercising, scheduling medical and dental appointments for yourself, and doing something for your emotional health every single day like enjoying a hobby, reading a book, or pursuing a goal that is important to you.

Some of these basic needs are sometimes put to the wayside when we are in a season of caring for others. We put everyone else's needs above our own. We neglect basic things like our personal appearance, our sleep, exercise, nutrition, doctor's appointments, and our mental health. We adopt the notion that it is okay to wear yoga pants all day with a messy bun and 4 days' worth of dry shampoo because we have kids to take care of and no time to shower or wash our hair.

I do love me some yoga pants and a messy bun every once in a while, and if that is truly your jam, then I am certainly not knocking it, but if you're choosing it because you say you have no time, then it's an excuse you need to lose right now.

You *have* the time to take a 10-minute shower, wash your hair, put on a little make-up and make yourself feel better. You *have* time to invest in yourself even if you're a mom of toddlers. Not having time is simply an excuse that busy moms like to use when it comes to self-care. I too am guilty of using it when it comes to certain things in my life that I know would make me feel and perform better. It's often much easier to make an excuse than it is to take action, right?

"I have no time to exercise, because I work, and I have kids."

"I haven't seen the dentist for a cleaning in years, because I can't take time off work."

"I know I'm due for a mammogram, but I can't find the time to do it, and I've heard that it's kind of painful."

"I would love to read more, but I just don't have time." (says the person who tells you about every new series on Netflix)

"My house is a hot mess, because I have no time to clean or organize it and hiring someone to help is too expensive."

"I wish I could eat healthy, but I don't have time to meal prep or cook healthy meals, because we live at the ballfield every night."

"I would love to go to the hair salon or get my nails done, but I don't have the time, nor do I feel like I should spend money on myself."

The truth is, we all have the time; we just have to arrange our time and our hours a little differently. We have to *make* the time for the things that are important to us and our overall health. We have to prioritize ourselves and what makes us feel our very best. We have to break the cycle of making endless excuses and instead choose to take action.

Our health matters.

Our personal appearance and the way it makes us feel matters.

Our quality of sleep matters.

Our mental and emotional health matters.

Filling our cup matters.

It matters so much that I'm writing an entire book about it.

I remember when I had my first baby. I was exhausted and sleep deprived and a bucket of tears at times, but I made sure to wake up every single day and shower, wash and fix my hair, put on a little make-up, and change into a cheerful outfit because it made me feel better. Just looking better made me feel better.

Even though I was still overwhelmingly tired, and my eyes could barely stay open some days, I felt clean and refreshed. I felt more like myself which was important to me. I felt somewhat normal in a stressful time when everything around me was new.

Fill up to Spill out

It didn't matter if I was leaving the house that day, if anyone was coming over or not, I still got myself ready for the day. I refused to give into the temptation of staying in my pajamas, not washing my hair or caring about my physical appearance just because I had a new baby.

When my second daughter came along less than 2 years later, I was exactly the same way. Whether I had to put her in a bouncer outside my shower door to keep her happy or had to wake up extra early to get it done, I made myself a priority. Yes, it is possible to shower every day even when you have a newborn, and you should want to.

Your physical appearance matters.

Not for the world, but for you.

A hot shower can make you feel like a million bucks. Fixing your hair, putting on a little make-up, and choosing an outfit that makes you feel good about yourself even when your body is all squishy and different can absolutely do wonders for your mood.

These are basic things, but so important. Neglecting your appearance, because you don't think you have time is telling yourself that you don't matter. But you do matter! And these things don't take that much time if you really think about it. I can get myself ready, and I mean like ready for work in 30 minutes flat. And this includes showering, washing and fixing my hair, putting on make-up and changing into an outfit that makes me feel pretty. 30 minutes. That's all. I'm serious. And I can do this, because I have a routine that works. I make quick work of it. I do it every day. And you can too!

You have the time. You just have to work it into your day. And if you have kids this requires planning ahead and waking up earlier. It involves prioritizing what matters and creating a consistent routine that works for you in your particular season.

Start by developing your own personal style and routine and stick with it. Wear what makes you feel good about yourself and keep it simple. Design your closet in a way that makes getting dressed in the morning feel easy and effortless.

I've built my wardrobe with different styles from a couple of brands I love, and my closet is organized, color-coded, and ready to go in the mornings. If you don't know how to do this, I would advise you to binge-watch multiple episodes of The Home Edit on Netflix. Pretty soon, everything in your house will have a system. Even my husband's side of the closet is now color-coded (even if he doesn't appreciate it).

In the mornings, I don't spend but a minute deciding what I am going to wear, because I know it all fits and goes together. I keep my accessories simple and classic. My necklaces are hanging on a rack for easy access. I don't have a ton of shoes, but instead a handful of comfy shoes I love. My make-up bag has just the essentials, and I make quick work out of putting my face on in the morning. I have a routine and do the same things in the same order every single morning. Boring? Maybe. But effective? Yes. I leave for work feeling put together and ready for the day ahead.

Consistency is key. How can you simplify things, adopt a style, and create an effortless system and routine that allows you to make your physical appearance a priority? Wouldn't it be nice to wake up in the morning and get yourself ready for the day before the day takes over?

When we are put together, we feel much better about ourselves. We have more confidence and security. We feel "normal." Right now, some of this normalcy has been stolen from us as our hair salons, nail salons and other services have been forced to close during Covid-19. We've gone months without a haircut, our roots are quite grown out, and our feet are not "summer ready." It has definitely given us a new sense of appreciation for our beloved services as we're being forced to go months without them. Looking good makes us feel good, and when we feel good, we tend to give our best.

If you're someone that has historically felt selfish for taking time to invest in your appearance, stop that right now. Make yourself a priority. Do it for you, but also for your daughters who are watching. Wake up earlier if you need to in order to take that shower and shave those legs. Take time to fix your hair and put on a little make-up. Invest in your wardrobe and organize your closet in a way that makes getting ready a cinch. Schedule regular hair appointments for yourself. Paint your nails each week or take time to go to the nail salon if you prefer a monthly mani/pedi. Develop a good skincare routine that your older self will thank you for. And be grateful for the person God made you to be. Treat her with loving care.

Not only does your physical appearance matter, but your physical health matters too. "If you don't make time for your wellness, be prepared to make time for your illness" (unknown).

Eating healthy meals, exercising, getting proper sleep, and going to regular check-ups is essential to maintaining our physical health, and we should make these things a priority. If we are not taking care of our body, we cannot take care of those around us. We might be able to get away with it for a little while, but sooner or later it catches up with us.

We eventually crash and burn, get sick, gain weight, develop medical conditions, and start feeling anxious, depressed, and tired. Sound familiar? In order to keep up with those around us, be at our best for those we love, do a good job at work, and be able to live a long healthy life, we have to focus on our physical health and wellness.

Right now, in the middle of this pandemic, our health probably matters more than anything else. Millions of people all over the globe are getting this virus and hundreds of thousands are dying from it. The virus seems to disproportionately affect people with poor immune systems and pre-existing medical conditions like obesity and diabetes. There is no better time to focus on improving our health than the present.

Nourishing our bodies with good wholesome food is essential to not just feeling out best but maintaining good overall health. When we are eating healthy proteins, fresh fruit and vegetables, and drinking plenty of water, our bodies get the proper nutrients needed to avoid getting sick and having long-term medical conditions like diabetes and heart disease. When we eat garbage, we start to feel like garbage. Processed foods with too much sugar and salt, fast-food and junk-foods, including our yummy lattes, not only add extra pounds to our bodies, but make us feel bad and eventually cause medical conditions to develop. We were not designed to eat this way, or at least not very often. Our bodies need clean healthy foods to flourish and feel our best. This requires planning and being intentional about what we are consuming most days.

Allison R. Smith

Eating healthy starts at home and requires a plan if we want it to actually happen. I have developed some systems and routines in our household that have helped us stay on track with meals. By no means are we perfect every day, because life happens, and sometimes we need Chick-fil-A, but having a plan definitely helps us stay organized and eat healthier most days.

Almost all of our meals come out of our home with the exception of eating out for a meal or two each week. On Sundays, I like to make out our weekly meal plan so that our busy evenings go smoother. I have a binder filled with a lot of our favorite meals and recipes, as well as a master grocery shopping list that can be hi-lighted each week before going to the store. Our pantry and fridge are organized in a way that makes meal preparation easy. Snacks are organized in baskets, and everything is taken out of its box and categorized so that it's easy to find. Meal-prepping isn't really our thing, but I do focus on meal planning, kitchen organization, and simplifying things to make our meal-times easier.

Our evenings are busy, but our meals are mostly healthy and on the table in usually less than 20 minutes. I take short-cuts wherever I can, not beating myself up about using prewashed salad or packaged shredded cheese, although the real stuff tastes better. Having about 20 easy meals that we rotate through each month like spaghetti, tacos, roasted salmon and vegetables, soups, fajitas, meatballs and mashed potatoes makes our evenings run smoothly. Plus, our girls are learning how to cook right there beside us. They will know how to prepare healthy meals for their own family someday, because time in the kitchen together is definitely time well spent.

Are you hoping to make meal-time easier? I would encourage you to start by taking control of your kitchen. Clean out and organize your pantry in a way that makes it functional and easier to stay on top of things. Keep staple items on hand and replace as needed. Use baskets to sort out your snacks, taking things out of their original boxing, and organizing like-things together. Do the same for your refrigerator and freezer. Just like having a system in your closet, having an organized space in your kitchen makes meal planning and preparing so much easier. Each week take your master grocery shopping list and hi-light the things you need to make grocery shopping a breeze. Order groceries online for pick-up if that helps you out. After all, it does save time and money, and you are less tempted to grab things you don't need. Sit down with your family and plan meals for the week. Prep any fruits and vegetables that can be prepped ahead of time. Take meats out of the freezer that need to be thawed before cooking. Brown up that meat if it can speed up your cooking time during the week.

It's all about getting ahead, setting yourself up for success during the workweek, and having a plan and a routine to keep your nutrition on track. Just because you live out at the ballfield doesn't mean you have to eat ballfield food every night. Eating healthy doesn't have to be complicated. A crock-pot meal or a simple sandwich with fresh fruit can be prepared in minutes and even enjoyed at the field.

Just like you have to have a plan for your nutrition, you also have to plan for regular exercise. Our bodies are made to move. And in a world where so many of our jobs involve sitting in front of a computer screen all day, we have to make time for movement.

I definitely feel my best when I am exercising every single day. Some days are definitely lighter, and other days I go on a long run, especially if I am training for something like a half marathon. But every day, I create time to get outside and move my body. I usually accomplish this by walking the dog in the morning before work, trying to get another quick walk in during my lunch break, and then going on a run in the evening. I also try and incorporate some strength training into my week as well, although I'll admit I'm more of a runner than anything else.

I love signing up for local races and doing at least 1-2 big races a year. Having a marathon or half-marathon to train for keeps me motivated to get my runs in. It makes it fun and rewarding. But running is not for everyone. Something like group fitness or cross-fit gyms might be your thing. Or maybe swimming or biking or hiking in nature. Whatever it is, be consistent and carve out that time for yourself each week. Choose to make physical activity an important part of your day, and I promise you won't regret it.

We feel so much better when we are exercising regularly. It's not only good for our heart, our joints, and our waistline, but it's also great for our emotional health. 30 minutes outside walking my dog or going for a run listening to good music is an instant mood-booster for me. Sometimes I don't feel motivated to do it, but when I choose to lace up my running shoes and do it anyways, I'm always glad I did.

Don't feel like you have time to exercise? Of course, you do! Again, it's all about creating a habit and a consistent routine that works for you. Decide that an active lifestyle is going to be part of your life. Visualize how it will feel to be active every single day and commit to doing it. You might find that you have to give up something in order to fit it in. Break it up into different time increments if you need to. Take a 10-minute walk before work, a 10-minute walk at lunch time, and then a 20-minute walk in the evening. Wake up an hour earlier and use that time to move your body. Skip the TV show at night and go for a run instead. Squeeze it in while you're watching your kid at soccer practice. Tell them you're getting in your exercise while they're getting in theirs. Trade off in the evenings with your spouse. You go for a run while he's cooking dinner and watching the kids, then he can go for a run after dinner.

My husband and I did that for several years when we were both training for marathons. It's called teamwork, and marriage is all about teamwork. Motivate each other by high fiving on your way in and his way out. Challenge each other to run more miles; push each other to get better. Or take the entire family out for an evening walk, run, or bike ride. Make it a family activity. Toss around a football while you walk together. I often see a family in our neighborhood doing that. It's all about creating a routine and sticking with it. Make it fun and enjoy the life-long reward of good health.

In the middle of this pandemic, I was feeling less motivated to run, especially in the hottest months of the year. I decided to challenge myself to run/walk 100 miles in August. I shared my commitment on social media and actually had several people including my husband join me for the challenge. For 31 days straight I laced up my shoes and put in over 3 miles a day on the roads.

There were no rest days or excuses, just consistency and forward progression towards a goal that I planned to crush. Even after a long day of work followed by a girl's night including a couple of drinks, I came home at 10:30pm and laced up my running shoes, grabbed a flashlight, and finished my miles for the day. I had made a commitment, and I wasn't about to break that promise to myself by missing one day. At the end of the month, my husband and I rolled over 100 miles, feeling accomplished and stronger. Pushing ourselves to complete this lofty goal gave us something else to focus on during a hard season filled with change.

If you're feeling less motivated to move your body, I would encourage you to challenge yourself to a goal each month. Commit to something like walking 2 miles a day, track your progress with your smart watch or phone, and celebrate your win.

Sleep is also an important part of your physical health. A good night's sleep is just as important as a healthy diet and regular exercise. In order to optimize your health and have energy to do get through your day, the average adult needs 6-8 hours of sleep every night. Invest in yourself by filling your cup with restful, restorative sleep.

If you're someone that has trouble sleeping at night make sure you are going to bed and waking up at the same time every day. I'd also encourage you to create a going to bed routine that helps you relax and get the sleep you need. Don't exercise or eat too late in the evening unless you want to deal with leg cramps or heartburn. Avoid caffeine too late in the day unless you like going to bed with a racing heart or the jitters.

Instead, take a hot bath or shower to relax your body. Create a cool, dark, and cozy sleeping environment. Use an oil diffuser, a sound machine, and fans to create the perfect room for sleep. Avoid watching TV or scrolling on your phone as tempting as it is. Instead, try reading a book or listening to soft music. Change your sheets often, because everyone knows clean sheets add to the awesomeness of your sleep environment. Try getting a new mattress or pillow if you wake up with neck or back pain. Good sleep is possible when you invest in your sleeping routine and environment.

And if you're a mom of a young baby right now, know that sleep is on its way. That 1st year is definitely filled with interrupted sleep and eyes that barely stay open, but do everything you can to get quality sleep, even if it's 2-3 hours at a time.

Has it been years since you had a wellness visit with lab work or a dental cleaning and check-up? Scheduling routine medical and dental appointments for yourself is so incredibly important when it comes to self-care. Neglecting to monitor your overall health can have detrimental effects. It's so much better to catch things before they become a big problem instead of waiting until it might be too late.

As a health care provider, I see this all too often. Some conditions are very treatable or even preventable with early detection. For example, breast cancer, cervical cancer, and colon cancer can all be detected early by getting your routine mammogram, pap smear, and colonoscopy when recommended. Even thyroid disease or even cancer can be detected by just having a physical exam.

Early in my career I noticed an enlarged thyroid in a seemingly healthy twenty-something year old female. After an ultrasound and then a biopsy, she was found to have thyroid cancer. Thankfully it was caught early enough, and she did well, but had she not come to see me that day, I'm not sure how long it would've gone unnoticed.

Your health is a priority, so get those appointments scheduled even if nothing feels wrong. See your health care provider like me at least once a year to go over your healthcare needs and see your dentist twice a year for dental cleanings and maintenance. Take your physical health seriously. It's all you have, especially in the middle of a pandemic.

Not only does your physical appearance and physical health matter, but your mental and emotional health matters too, maybe more than anything else. Because if your head's not right, you're not going to do any of these other things, right?

Mental illnesses are unfortunately amongst the most common health conditions we see in our country. Almost half of adults will

Fill up to Spill out

experience mental illness in their lifetime. It's important that we take an active role in managing our own mental and emotional health by finding ways to bring peace and joy to our lives each day. Stress, struggle, and loss is going to happen, but how we react and respond to life's ups and downs is what's important. We have to learn to cope with these things in healthy ways. We must figure out what makes us feel calm, grounded, and fulfilled, and do more of those things every single day.

I've mentioned that exercise can be a huge mood-booster. Getting outside and going for a run is free therapy for me. It's worship, time in nature, sunshine, and alone-time. It makes me really happy. It brings me peace. And maybe it does the same for you. I also love reading non-fiction, listening to Christian music, writing and blogging, journaling, taking beautiful pictures of flowers and nature, walking my dog, getting creative, cleaning and organizing my space, and I love traveling to new places and checking out the local coffee shops and wineries wherever I go. I do most of these things in one way or another every single day. I know what fills me up, and I make filling up with peace and joy a priority.

What is it that fills you up when you're feeling down? How do you choose to fill your cup whether life is great or not so great? I'd encourage you to spend some time thinking about the things that truly make you happy and bring peace and joy to your life. Everyone should have a list, and there should be at least 10 things on that list. Go ahead and write them down and start pursuing these things on a regular basis.

Obviously, I can't travel to new places every day, but I can most certainly plan for a trip once or twice a year if going to the beach or the mountains is what brings me joy. I can also enjoy drinking my coffee on the patio in the morning, walking the dog in the evening as the sun goes down, reading a good book with a glass of wine, going for a long run, listening to a podcast, or taking a long shower. It's all about discovering the things that help you stay grounded and calm and making time for them every single day. Self-care is not selfish when it makes us show up as a better person. Everyone needs to take time to do things that bring them joy.

Allison R. Smith

I am always surprised when I hear moms in my office tell me that they never take time to do things they enjoy. Either they feel like they don't have time, or they feel guilty for using their time on themselves. They just go through the motions every day of working and taking care of the kids, their spouse, and their home, never taking an hour or half-hour to do something that fills them up.

It's no wonder that they feel empty.

It's no wonder they feel anxious or depressed.

It's no wonder they feel so overwhelmed and stressed out.

Everyone needs time for themselves, no matter what season they are in. Whether you are a working mom or stay-at-home mom, a married mom or a single mom, you deserve to have time to do something each day that fills your cup. You deserve an hour to yourself, whether it's for exercise, reading, taking a bath while listening to music and sipping a glass of wine, or organizing your closet.

Wake up early, stay up late; just do what you have to do to gain a little time for yourself. Make it a priority, and I promise your mental health will thank you.

Covid-19 has caused a significant rise in mental health issues. If it's not the fear and concern over the virus itself, it's the change and isolation as a result of social distancing or the loss of jobs and businesses that has unfortunately led to more depression, anxiety, insomnia, and even suicide. The situational stress is felt by almost everyone. All of our lives are being affected in one way or another, and some days are really hard.

It's all about how we choose to react and respond to the change, fear, and isolation that's important. This virus isn't going away, or at least not anytime soon. Stress and loss are never completely going away, much to our disappointment. 2020 feels hard, but I bet we've all gone through something more difficult. And if not, know that life is going to continue to throw us curveballs, but it's still possible to learn how to hit them out of the park.

We have to learn how to manage our stress. We have to create a life that focuses on cultivating peace, hope, joy, and purpose. This looks like regular exercise, getting outside in nature, taking time for ourselves to do things we enjoy, having a creative outlet, consuming positive content, and connecting with a community that lift us up when we're feeling down. Prayer and journaling that includes a daily gratitude practice can also be quite helpful.

I would recommend trying some different things. Develop some routines and habits that work for you. Create time for yourself, even if you have to wake up an hour or two earlier. Pursue personal growth and I bet that your mental and emotional health will greatly improve.

And if these things don't seem to be working for you, don't hesitate to get professional help. As a health care provider, I prescribe medications for depression and anxiety and refer patients for counseling almost every single day. It's a huge part of what I do, and I love taking care of women like me. We're in this life together, and there are lots of us who want to help.

Don't feel shame in asking for help. You deserve to feel your best in a body that is healthy and emotionally stable, and there are professionals who can help you reach your goals of being your very best self.

As I wrap up this chapter, I would encourage you to take some time to evaluate your calendar, routines and habits. Do you currently spend time investing in self-care, or is your life filled with endless work, chores, and kid's activities? Do you have an early morning routine that grounds you and sets you up for success, or do you rush to get out of the door on time each day? Do you make time for exercise? Meal prepping? Passions and hobbies? Do you create time for yourself to invest in yourself?

Now find at least one hour a day that you can focus on filling your cup with things that bring you joy, because you are worth it! Schedule your exercise, plan your meals, get those check-ups on the calendar for the year, and make your health a priority. Focus on nutrition, exercise, sleep, and your mental health. Read books or listen to podcasts to grow your knowledge on these topics. Build habits that keep you grounded even when times are stressful.

Covid-19 is definitely testing us in many ways right now. If you had great habits before, are you keeping up with them? If you had bad habits before this pandemic, are you using this time to create better ones? This time could be the gift you needed to reevaluate your priorities, focus on much-needed self-care, and become an even stronger, healthier version of yourself.

I love this quote by Dave Hollis during quarantine, "In the rush to return to normal, use this time to consider which parts of normal are worth rushing back to."

We are all so ready to get back to "normal" after weeks and months of experiencing what is not "normal." But what are we going to rush back to if and when things get back to the way they used to be? What do we miss and what are we going to change? Are we going to keep pouring into everyone else neglecting our own health and needs? Or are we going to start filling up with self-care, so we have more to spill out to those around us?

Chapter 2

Fill up with order & simplicity

"You can't experience simple joys when you're living life with your hair on fire."

Emily Ley

My husband has been a school administrator for many years and is currently serving as a middle school principal. He has often described what he does, including his daily tasks and decision making, as "putting out fires." From the moment he steps foot on his campus each day, he is making one decision after another, extinguishing fires as they arise, often interrupted by various people throughout the day. With not enough hours in the workday, he often misses lunch and he frequently brings work home. He works hard, but he also feels passionate about what he does, trying to do it a little bit better each day, putting systems into place that hopefully prevent little fires from turning into big ones. A lot of us feel passionate about what we do, whether we work outside the home or stay at home with little ones. And just like my husband, we can sometimes feel like we are putting out fires all day long, or maybe we actually feel like we're the ones with our hair on fire needing to stop, drop, and roll.

If you're a busy mom like me, you're walking through a season of life that is full of constant demands from everyone and everything. Work, kids, a spouse, family, friends, pets, and our homes and all the things in them are constantly competing for our attention. There are forms to be filled out, lunches to be made, meetings to attend, bills to be paid, and chores to be done. If it's not a sick kid, it's a sick pet. If it's not something at work, it's a flat tire or perhaps a leak in the roof at home. There's always something. The question is, how do we find time for ourselves and keep our lives running smoothly when all we feel like we are doing is stomping out fires every day? How do we take care of them before they turn into massive forest fires or better yet, how do we prevent them in the first place?

As a working mom, I've been trying to figure this out for years, as I want to give my best to those around me without feeling like I'm always depleted. And what I've learned is that we can't do a good job without spending some time creating order, routines, habits, and simplicity in our lives. No one benefits from a frazzled, disorganized, unprepared mom, wife, friend, or worker.

If we are always showing up late to work, unkempt and unprepared, we are probably going to lose our job, right? Just as important as it is to show up well for our jobs, we must show up well for ourselves and those around us. This means we have to learn some ways to prepare and create order and harmony in our homes and in our lives, develop routines and habits that work, and

Fill up to Spill out

simplify areas of our life that allow us to be more productive and feel less drained. The more organization we pour into our cup, the smoother everything flows out.

Before my nursing career, like a lot of my college friends including my husband, I waited tables at a local country club. If you've done it yourself, you know how demanding it is to be a waiter or waitress. And if you've been a customer at a restaurant, you know that having a good waiter versus a bad one can mean the difference between a great dining experience versus a not-so-great one, right?

It's an important job. Being a good waitress requires arriving early, being prepared, developing friendliness and consistency, and learning how to prioritize. I quickly figured out that if I arrived early to make sure all the ice bins were full, the lemons were washed and cut, the tea and coffee were made, the napkins were folded just right, and everything was ready to go before the customers started arriving, I had a much smoother shift. I was good at my job because I hustled and did the prep-work, I had a consistent routine, and I learned how to multi-task as I took care of all my tables. It was a great experience for me.

When I think about it, I probably first learned a lot of these skills from watching my mom and grandma growing up. Everything for the holidays was always prepared ahead of time, making it stress-free for the guests arriving for the day. We'd walk through the door of my grandparent's house and everything was literally done. There was a huge spread of food across the island in their kitchen, homemade pies waiting to be eaten, and beautiful tables covered in tablecloths with carefully folded napkins and silverware. Fresh flowers and lit candles added to the holiday atmosphere. Cups full of ice were waiting to be filled with tea, and her house was always so welcoming (except for the thermostat set on 78, quickly to be turned down as we all arrived).

My grandma took such pride in hosting family meals and gatherings. She prepared weeks ahead of time in order to not make the day of the event so stressful. Like my grandma, my mom has always been good about making sure everything is nice and ready as our families start to arrive for the holidays or special events. The tables are set, the dessert is made, and the meal is always delicious. I'm so glad I learned from the best. I don't think I would have been as good of a waitress (or a wife and mom) had I not learned the importance of preparing ahead of time.

When I began working on a busy hospital unit, I used some of these same skills to become a great nurse. I arrived early, I did the prep-work to make sure I knew all about the patients I would be caring for during my shift, the tasks I needed to accomplish each hour for the 5 or so patients under my care, and anything else I needed to plan for.

I began seeing patients using my carefully written out guide for the day, systematically doing the tasks I needed to do, while remaining quick on my feet when problems arose. No day was the same, and by no means was any day perfect, but I always felt like I was prepared for whatever was going to come my way. Being a nurse sometimes felt like being a glorified waitress in many ways. Instead of refilling drinks, serving food, and cleaning off tables, I was handing out pills, performing nursing skills, and turning and cleaning patients all day. I learned to be quick on my feet while doing it all with a smile on my face.

It wasn't but about 6 months or so into my nursing career that I was promoted to charge nurse. At the tender age of 22 or so, I became a leader on my unit, making assignments for other nurses, overseeing the flow of the floor, signing off doctor's orders, and reporting off to the next charge nurse. I was leading people that were twice my age, which was absolutely crazy. It was eye-opening and quite stressful at times, but definitely a great learning experience. Looking back on it now I realize that we're often pushed into those uncomfortable positions that we're not really ready for in order to grow us into who we are becoming.

After going back to school for 3 years while working on my floor, I transitioned into my current role of family nurse practitioner over 12 years ago. My job is much different now as I work in a provider role alongside the physicians, but I still use a lot of the same guiding principles to do my current job in a clinic setting. I always arrive early to prepare for the day ahead, I have systems and routines that guide my work-flow, I prioritize what needs to be done now versus what can wait until the end of the day, and I've learned simple tricks to get things done more efficiently so I can get home to my family at the end of the day. I love my work, but I love my family more, so making sure I get home on time is always a priority.

As a working mom, I stay busy. And if you're also in this season with me or were there not long ago, you can definitely relate. There are kids to care for and get to all the places, work to be done, a mountain of laundry every week, a dishwasher that never stops, groceries to buy, meals to prepare, errands to run, a dog to walk, a house to clean, and the list could go on and on right?

It's exhausting just listing all the endless tasks that we do during this busy season of working and raising kids. Certain areas of our life often get neglected when life starts to feel overwhelming. Chores start to pile up, car and home maintenance and repairs tend to be ignored, everything feels chaotic, and before long we start to feel the weight of it all. We feel like our days and our lives are spinning out of control, and there's no end in sight. We are no longer putting out fires, but instead the fires are consuming us. We no longer feel in control, but instead like we are being controlled by the chaos. Does this sound familiar?

This is why we need to create order and simplicity. Life doesn't have to be so overwhelming all the time. We don't have to do everything or be everything to everyone, if you know what I mean. There's a better way. We can say no. We can decide what's important, saying yes to the things that truly matter and heck no to the things that don't. We can regain control by discovering ways to create harmony in both our homes and in our lives.

When you live a busy (and sometimes stressful) life like I do, you have to start by getting organized. I suppose it can be fun to live carefree, taking one day at a time, one hour at a time, and being spontaneous and all, but when you are someone that has kids and a job and a home and a thousand responsibilities, you have to be prepared. There is no other way. You have to be intentional about how you plan your days and plan your year. You should not only know what's going on today, but what's happening 6 months or even a year from now.

Where I work, patients can book appointments up to a year in advance. I need to be able to tell my manager when I will be taking vacation and when I have special events to attend months and months in advance. I need to know when my husband will be out of town, I need to know when he has late nights at work, and I need to know who is taking the girls to all of their things.

This looks different for everyone, but I have multiple calendars that I use to keep me and everyone in my household aware of what's going on. I know a lot of people use electronic calendars on their device, but I still prefer old fashioned paper calendars and planners to stay organized. I like seeing the big picture, writing out my plans, and crossing off days as they pass. I have a large desk calendar at home, one at work, and I keep a planner in my purse. I keep all 3 updated at all times, so I can look ahead no matter where I am. On any given day, I can see that it's a field trip day, we have piano or soccer practice in the evening, and we are having spaghetti for dinner. I can see in 3 months that I have a hair appointment and the girls have their dentist appointments. I can see that in 6 months we are taking a family vacation... yippee! Everything is there for the family to see, and we all know what to plan for. Planning is the key to avoiding unexpected fires. No one likes to be surprised, unless maybe it's a good surprise like you won a trip to Disneyworld. One can dream.

I'm not sure how anyone can function without some sort of calendar, daily planner, or system in their home. Failing to plan or stay organized is setting yourself up for missed doctor's appointments, forgetting to send the sack lunch for the kid's field trip, or not having a clue what's for dinner at the end of a busy day. We've all been there. #momfail. We forgot picture day. We forgot about the spelling test, and therefore our kid bombed it. We missed the birthday party and feel horrible about it. We arrive home only to realize that there's nothing in the fridge for dinner.

Staying on top of all the things requires planning and organization and developing a system that works for you. That might look like writing on old-school paper calendars and planners like me, using the calendar on your smart phone and setting alerts and reminders each day, or using a big dry erase board in your home. Everyone needs to be on the same page. Communication is crucial. When there are lots of moving parts each day, each member of the family needs to know what's going

Fill up to Spill out

on, who's picking up who, what's for dinner, what chores or errands need to be done, and so on. An organized home is a smoothly run home.

Creating order also involves establishing roles and responsibilities for each family member. Who is responsible for what? If you are married, you need to establish early on who is mostly in charge of the daily, weekly, and monthly tasks that need to be done to keep a home running seamlessly and where you're going to enlist some help.

In our home, I am blessed to work 4 days a week, allowing a day off during the week to get most of the cleaning, laundry, and errands done. I do some tidying and laundry on other days, but on my day off I tackle the bigger cleaning and chores. My husband takes care of the finances in our home, making sure the bills get paid and our taxes get done correctly. He also takes care of car and home repairs and manages our rental property. We often share in the evening cooking and dishes, depending on who gets home first, and our girls are responsible for some chores as well. We take the help when it comes to our yard. It's worth every penny to have someone come and mow our yard each week so my husband doesn't have to spend hours of our weekend doing it. In this season of life, he has a super busy job with lots of responsibilities, so having that help with our yard has been a lifesaver.

If I didn't have a day off during the week, I would most definitely consider hiring a cleaning lady. Working 5 days a week with kids and all their activities is craziness. If you can afford to get help with the house or yard, even just once or twice a month, definitely do it. It's money well spent, and valuable time you can spend doing something else that fills your cup.

There is absolutely no shame in asking for help. Women are busier now than ever before. Our houses and yards are much larger than they used to be. Do yourself a favor and hire some help if you need it. A clean and cozy home along with a well-maintained yard are so important in keeping your life in order. As Gretchen Rubin says in one of her books, "outer order contributes to inner calm." I couldn't agree more. I am definitely someone that requires a clean and tidy space in order to not feel anxious.

I encourage you to create a system and a daily and weekly routine that works for you and your family in your particular season. Make quick work of the chores, turn on some music, make it fun, and create much-needed order in your home. Decide what needs to be done each week or every other week, write it down, break it up into certain days or if you have an entire day to devote to chores, knock it all out in one day. I don't know about you, but when I am surrounded by a mess, I feel like a mess. Our physical surroundings can have tremendous power over our mental and emotional health. A clean, organized, and welcoming home can bring such peace and joy to our very busy life, filling our cup so we can spill out to others.

We tend to become the person we are through our routines and habits.
John C. Maxwell says "You'll never change your life until you change something you do daily. The secret of your success is found in your daily routine."

Daily habits have the potential to either fuel us or absolutely drain us. If we want to live a life full of purpose, showing up for those around us in the best way possible, functioning at a high level without feeling like we are always on empty, we must create habits and routines that serve us.

In my opinion, morning routine is everything. How we start our day is how our day will go. When I wake up late and barely have enough time to get myself ready before getting the kids up and ready for school only to realize that lunches haven't been made and my daughter can't find her shoes, and we barely get out the door on time, I know my day is already going to be bad.

Thankfully that hasn't happened in years, but does this sound familiar to you? Do you barely give yourself enough time to get dressed in the morning before the kids wake up? Or do the kids actually wake you up in the morning? How is that working for you? Do you feel frazzled, anxious, and already a hot mess express before your day even begins? Do you wonder why everyone is so irritable? Or why you're always late? Why you never seem to have a moment to yourself to just drink your coffee in peace? Mornings don't have to be that way.

Now picture yourself getting up at least an hour earlier, having some quiet time to yourself to enjoy a delicious cup of hot coffee on the patio, spend time reading, journaling, or getting in a 30-minute work-out. This is followed by a nice shower and getting yourself ready before waking up the kids, eating breakfast together, grabbing all the lunches and items that have been prepared the night before, and leaving for work and school on time, excited about the day ahead. Doesn't that sound better than the frantic morning I mentioned before? Wouldn't a morning routine filled with good habits serve you and your family well?

Creating a morning routine starts the night before. Set yourself up for success by preparing lunches for the following day, setting out clothes especially if you plan on exercising in the morning, getting the coffee maker ready for brewing, setting your alarm, and going to bed on time. In order to wake up early, you have to go to bed earlier. Skip the late-night news or Netflix show and instead create an ideal sleeping environment that allows you to get 7-8 hours of sleep. You can't expect to wake up at 5am if you go to bed too late. Train your body to be a morning person by not being a night owl.

When morning comes and that alarm goes off, don't overthink it, but just get up. Once you're upright and physically leaving the room, you'll be less likely to go back to sleep. No snoozing, no hesitating; just roll out of bed. If you're needing more motivation to get up early in the morning, read books like The Miracle Morning by Hal Elrod or The 5 Second Rule by Mel Robins. Those books changed my life.

Give yourself a big enough reason to get up before you have to. Create a morning routine that is so rewarding that you look forward to it every single day. Your "why" has to be strong. Your reason for getting up an hour or two earlier has to be powerful. Having that time to invest in yourself, pursue a goal, get ahead for the day, or just have some much-needed peace and quiet before the chaos is why you are waking up early. Make that time so valuable that you are not even slightly tempted to push the snooze button when that alarm goes off in the morning.

Last year I started waking up at 4:30am in order to write my first book. As a working mom, that was the only time I could find in my day, so I made it work. My goal of finishing my book by the end of the year kept me motivated to keep waking up early. Day after day I woke up nearly 2 hours earlier than the rest of the house in order to get my word-count in. I used that time to pursue a goal that was important to me. My "why" kept me going even when I was tired and wanted to sleep in. I'd start by sipping some coffee and writing in my journal, and then I would get after it on the keyboard, one word at a time, once chapter at a time, and by the end of the year, I had a finished manuscript. While my family slept, I wrote, and I loved every minute of it. So much, that I'm doing it again!

That's what it takes to create a morning routine. You have to make it so productive and satisfying that you actually look forward to it. What is it that you want? Do you want more time to yourself? Are you searching for time to get your work-out in? Do you want to be able to read more? Write a book? Go back to school? Have more time to read your Bible and pray? Work on a side hustle? Or do you just want to be able to sip your coffee and watch the beautiful sunrise before the kids wake up and all the chaos begins? There's nothing wrong with that! If you're a busy mom like me, the early morning hours are the perfect time to pour into your cup. That time is actually the favorite part of my day now.

Commit to waking up early. Try it for 30 days, and I bet you'll keep doing it. Work on creating daily habits that serve you well. Not only will you see the benefits, but your family will also reap the rewards. Pour into yourself so you can spill out to others. Model to your kids what it looks like to start your day with intention. Show them how to also set their day up for success by preparing the night before.

Provide a peaceful environment with less rush and more joy in the morning. Allow more time for them to wake up before rushing off to school. Be prepared for the day ahead. Choose positivity. I promise you won't regret starting your day earlier, but you'll always regret being late.

There are other great habits and routines that are also essential to living a more intentional life filled with more joy and less rush and chaos. Creating a habit of making your bed every day is a great place to start. I love leaving the house feeling like it's tidy and ready to come home to after a long day. It's so much nicer getting into a fresh bed at night. Not leaving dishes in the sink is also a great habit. Taking the time to go ahead and load and start the dishwasher at night makes it so much nicer to walk into the kitchen in the morning. It's the same thing with the washer and dryer. Try to make it a habit to go ahead and fold and put away the clothes as soon as they're done drying. Clothes that pile up in the basket end up wrinkled and never seem to get put away. (I used to be guilty of this, but it's definitely happening less often.) Recruit some help with this from the kids. My oldest daughter is a great help with folding the laundry while watching a movie. I was the same way when I was growing up.

On Sundays my husband likes to fill up our cars with gas and also run them through the carwash to start our week off right. It sure does feel good getting into a clean car on Monday and not having to worry whether there's gas in the tank or not. It's all about creating habits and routines that make your life easier. Little things can make a huge difference!

As we seek more order and less chaos, we must also learn to simplify. Emily Ley is a great resource in this area and has some really helpful and esthetically beautiful books you can check out on simplifying every area of your life. The point is that life doesn't have to be so complicated. We don't have to say yes to everything. We can say no to the things that don't spark peace, joy, or purpose. We can leave some weekends completely open on our calendars (there's been a lot of that with Covid!). We can celebrate birthdays without all the hoopla. We can take short cuts in the kitchen to save time. Not every meal has to be elaborate. It's okay to buy the prewashed bagged salad or the already prepared frozen meatballs to save time and energy in the kitchen. We can also get rid of all the clutter and excess, just focusing on the things we need and love. We can get back to simple and basic.

Coronavirus has most definitely forced us to get back to simple. Any prior commitments we had suddenly no longer exist. There's no rushing from work and school to soccer practice or gymnastics or piano. There are literally zero activities outside of our essential jobs and some virtual schooling from home. Our evenings and weekends are strangely quiet, allowing for family walks and bike rides in the neighborhood, board games, puzzles, and rewarding home projects. We have time for yard work and fishing at the creek. We are cooking all of our meals at home, with the exception of some occasional take-out, mostly to support our local small businesses.

We are baking cookies, redecorating rooms, organizing closets, and watching old movies every night before bedtime. Special events have been reduced to much smaller gatherings. We are spending less money on things like entertainment, services, travel, and gas. It suddenly feels like there are more hours in the day, even if we are still working during this pandemic. It's actually pretty great.

I was already on a simplifying kick as I started 2020, but the pandemic has really forced me to reevaluate all areas of our life. Every room, closet, and cabinet in our house is being decluttered, cleaned, and organized. I am painting and changing out photos and decor, giving the house a fresh simple updated look. It's giving me a sense of purpose during all this craziness, while also serving to simplify our space. I'm taking time to reevaluate how we were previously spending all of our time. I have always been someone that likes to be busy, but this new slower pace has also been nice. Having free weeknights and weekends is actually a blessing. It's really giving us more time to relax and enjoy each other's company. As we come out of this pandemic, and life starts to return to normal or a new sense of normal, I will definitely reconsider what goes back on our calendar.

What areas of your life do you need to create order and simplify? Do you need to work on developing a better morning routine that sets your day up for success? Do you need to get your house cleaned and organized to produce more calm in your life? Do you need to go out and buy some old-fashioned paper calendars like me to plan for the upcoming year? Or do you need to ask for some help?

Women are notorious for not wanting to ask for help. We think we can do it all and do it all well, but the truth is that no one can truly do it all or at least not do it all well. If hiring a cleaning lady or a yard service or an assistant would help to add joy and harmony to your life, don't feel shame in getting some help. Lighten the load where you can. Simplify your life, establish routines and habits that serve you and your family well, and create some space for free weeknights and weekends at home. Make time to fill your cup, and I bet you'll feel less frazzled.

Allison R. Smith

Chapter 3

Fill up with community

> *"Alone, we can do so little; together we can do so much."* Helen Keller

My parents have an old boat that unfortunately sits in storage most of the year. It's a good-looking deck boat with lots of open space making it great for families and friends to enjoy a day at the lake. However, it's not the most reliable boat in town. That's the thing about boats; they always need to go into the shop. The best kind of boat is the boat that isn't yours; the boat that you just hop on, enjoy, and hand over some gas money for a fun time on the water. Boats always need work, especially the ones that sit in storage most of the year.

Allison R. Smith

My husband Ted and I have probably used this boat more than my parents or the rest of the family over the last decade or two, taking friends out on the lake in our town to tube, ski, and swim. Ted didn't grow up driving boats or backing up trailers while living in Houston, so it was always an adventure when we decided to go out on the lake during those early years of our marriage. One thing he would frequently forget was to replace the plug before putting the boat on the water.

I recall one beautiful day out at the lake when I discovered water coming into the boat as we were floating along getting things ready for tubing. Water inside a boat meant something was terribly wrong, so I mentioned it to my husband, while trying to remain calm. His hazel eyes grew big, as he frantically started the boat (that rarely started on the first time) and sped up trying to run the water out before jumping into the lake to put the plug back in. I never realized how important that little plug was until not having it in almost caused our boat to sink. It was sort of a running joke after that, as we asked him each time we went out to the lake, "hey Ted, did you remember the plug?" Sometimes a little scare like that is what it takes to make you realize the importance of something.

Just like our boat needs that plug to keep it afloat, we need community to hold us up. We need family and friends to fill our cup with laughter, energy, and support. We need people who add value to our lives and make it fun. We need date nights with our hubby, girl's nights with our friends, daily walks with our neighbors, camaraderie at work, and special gatherings with our family. We need to invest our time in others and be invested in as well.

As an introvert and someone that is very independent, it really does not bother me to be alone. I often crave "alone time," especially during this busy season of life when I am surrounded by people most of the day. As a healthcare provider listening to people basically complain all day (looking for solutions of course), my work has a tendency to drain me. I look forward to moments where I can be by myself to fill my cup. Being alone is probably what recharges me more than anything else.

Fill up to Spill out

I'm one of those people that loves cleaning and organizing my house listening to music or a podcast as I go room to room with my cleaning supplies. Being home alone doesn't bother me. It's actually kind of amazing these days. I'm also someone that prefers running alone, going at my own pace, enjoying the solitude and the freshness of the clean crisp air. I often do my best thinking when I'm running alone. Most of what I post online and write in my books are words that were written in my head on a run and later taken to the keyboard. I also enjoy walking our dog and just getting out in nature to process my feelings.

I'm not someone that's afraid to go to work conferences alone or even stay in hotels alone. I don't mind eating alone or shopping alone. In fact, I kind of prefer it. The thought of slowly walking down every beautiful aisle at Target or Marshall's with a Starbuck's drink in my hand just sounds like Heaven to me. Sometimes we need some alone time. We need peace and quiet without any distractions or interruptions to rest and recharge or to just be productive. Alone time is good, and we should want some every day.

But we also need community. We need real people in our lives that help us to become a better version of ourselves. God didn't create us to be alone, but to find community to connect with and learn from, to be vulnerable with and grow with, to encourage and be encouraged by. We are better together. We need to fill our cup with quality time with our spouse, sweet friendships, work friends, groups with common interests and goals, family who are also friends, as well as a church community.

Connections are important. Life is about lifting one another up, having fun together, and sharing life's up and downs with each other. Life is about loving God and loving others. It's not just about loving ourselves (which some of us are quite good at) but loving other people. Jesus was sent to show us how to love one another. He was all about people, and not just some people, but *all* people. When we build community and love on each other, we are becoming more and more like Jesus. And shouldn't that be our ultimate purpose?

Coronavirus is trying to take community away from us. We are being told to stay at home, quarantine, and only leave to go to our essential jobs and pick up essential items from the store. Every large public event and gathering that brings community together has literally been cancelled. Even churches have closed their doors indefinitely, switching to all virtual services. We miss community. We miss our friends and family. We miss gathering in our church building to worship with other believers. Our kids miss going to school with their friends and playing sports and doing all their activities.

Doing life alone can be lonely. We are starting to realize how much we need community now that we are being forced to live without it. Yes, we are learning how to connect virtually with others and watch church from our phones, but it's definitely not the same thing. We need community in the aspect of real-life connections, hugs, handshakes, and intimate conversations. We need people in our lives.

I've had the same email account for nearly 20 years. I depend on it for nearly everything, so you can imagine how panicked I felt when I could not access my email account for several days in a row during this pandemic. For some reason, I got kicked out, and my login and password would no longer work. I spent an exhausting amount of time and effort trying to reset my password with no success. Apparently, my email had been bought out by another company making it even more difficult to get some help. I tried calling email assistance only to get a very frustrating computer-generated answering service that I couldn't get anywhere with. I felt incredibly tense, frustrated, and worried by the whole ordeal. I had saved emails that I needed to get access to. This email address was used for literally everything. I desperately continued to try to find someone who could help me.

And then one beautiful morning, I called the number that usually took me to the computer-generated service, and an actual person answered the phone. It took me by surprise. An actual person. A friendly voice on the other end of the line was the angel I had been praying for. She reassured me she could help, and 45 minutes later the sweet lady was finally able to get me into my email again. In a world filled with technology, technology couldn't fix my technology problem, but a real-life person could. Bless that real-life person that helped me in my stressful time of need.

Fill up to Spill out

We need people. We don't just need virtual friends, but real-life genuine friends.

As we journey through life, we will have friends for different seasons, but we will also form some long-lasting friendships for a much bigger reason. These are the friendships that stand the test of time, moves, disappointment, and loss. We don't need a lot of friends, but we need some really great ones like this. We need friends who we can gather with to celebrate life's wins but also to mourn the losses with. We need friends we can truly be vulnerable with, friends who get us, friends who will just listen and not say a single word; friends who can give solid advice when needed and not just their opinion. We need friends we can count on when times are great, but also when times are not so great.

I truly have the best group of friends. My tribe has been such a blessing to me over the years. These friends are like family, and I can't imagine going through life without them. We've gone through a lot over the years, but our friendship has definitely stood the test of time and change. Our husbands are friends, our kids are friends, and it's been so special to watch our families grow up together. Summer wouldn't feel like summer if it weren't for our annual beach trips together. Our weekends wouldn't be as much fun without our girl's nights or gatherings at each other's houses. My phone would be much quieter if it weren't for all our group text messages. Celebrations wouldn't be as sweet. Hard times would be harder if we didn't lift each other up. Through all of life's ups and downs, twists and turns, I am truly grateful for my tribe of friends.

But it's not just our close-knit group of friends that make life more fun, but the community we find in other places too. After all, people are everywhere, and we need to seek out other ways to love and connect with people.

We spend a tremendous amount of our day with the people we work with. 40-60 hours a week are sometimes spent with this community of people with a common mission. We might not necessarily have a best friend at work, but we definitely have friends that make work more fun. I'd encourage you to get to know your co-workers. Take a genuine interest in who they are, what they like, and treat them how you wish to be treated. Work together to form a great team. After all, teamwork is definitely the dreamwork. We can't do our jobs well without a great team. Spend time together outside of work. Do nice things for your work friends. Be the one that shows up with the donuts on a Friday. Be the one that decorates a desk for a birthday. Be the one who always smiles and says thank you. Create the environment you desire to be a part of, and I bet you'll like your job a lot more.

When I started my nursing career on an intimidating floor in the hospital, it was the team that I worked with who kept me on that crazy busy floor for over 5 years. My plan was to never stay there, but instead transfer to a women's health or neonatal floor as soon as something opened up. But my team changed my plans as they quickly went from being my co-workers to becoming my friends and greatest mentors. We were a rock-star team that couldn't be knocked down. Tough shifts were made easier because we could count on one another for help. We turned hard work into fun times and big tears into laughter.

Nursing is definitely not a glamorous job, especially when you work on a floor like I did. 12-hour days are filled with turning and cleaning up adult patients (so many wipes and bed changes), lifting and bending, silencing IV pumps, answering call lights, and going home with an aching back, swollen feet, and sometimes a broken heart. My husband used to joke with me when I'd talk in my sleep at night, hearing dinging IV pumps and beeping call lights, worried that I had forgotten to do something during my shift. It wasn't unusual for me to call up to my floor late at night to tell the next shift something that I had forgotten to include in my report. I'm still friends with a lot of those nurses many years later after leaving the floor for my next career as a nurse practitioner. I honestly wouldn't be where I am today had I not been inspired and encouraged by those incredible nursing friends on STC-3.

Our neighbors are also an important part of our community of friends. Do you know the people you share a fence with? Have you friended the people who walk their dogs alongside you every night? If you haven't, then you are missing out on a wonderful opportunity to find community right across the street. Your new best friend could be next door. Or at least maybe they're someone who could keep an eye on your house or watch your dog for you while you are gone.

Neighborhoods sure have changed a lot over the years. When I was growing up, our neighbors were our best friends. My parents would tell us to go outside and play, and we'd often be found next door or just down the street playing with the kids in our neighborhood. They didn't worry about us (or least it didn't feel that way) unless we didn't make it home by dinner time. Our neighbors would welcome us into their homes like we were one of their own kids. It was great.

But the times have certainly changed, and neighborhoods have also changed. People are busier with their jobs and kid's activities and tend to keep more to themselves these days. Parents are more afraid of letting their kids play in the front yard. And I don't blame them, as I am one of those parents too. The world is a different place. But it doesn't mean that you can't be kind to your neighbors.

A simple gesture like saying hello, waving as they pass by, chatting in the yard, picking up their newspaper, returning their trash dumpster to where it belongs, and learning their dog's name goes a long way. These simple ways of being kind to your neighbor can be the beginning of a beautiful friendship. Don't shy away from getting to know the people around you. They are often looking for friends too. And pretty soon you'll be drinking wine together in the driveway or dog-sitting for each other when you go out of town.

Our family is also a huge part of the community we do life with. If you are lucky enough to live near your family, then most likely you gather with them often. My grandma was always so great about rallying the troops for all the important holidays and birthdays. We loved going to my grandparent's house when we were growing up. It meant we would get to see our cousins from out of town, we'd get to build forts and put on music and theatre performances, eat pie and play dominoes. I have such fond memories of circling around the kitchen to pray before a giant spread of food, eating and playing late into the night. It was loud and crazy, and I'm sure we left a giant mess for my grandma but being together was always so much fun.

Allison R. Smith

Just like I grew up going to my grandparent's house for holidays and birthdays, my girls get to make those same memories at my parent's house now. They still live in the same house I grew up in out in the country, and my two brothers and their families live nearby. Living only two towns away, we get to see my parents quite often. My girls look forward to going to their grandparent's house to swim and play with their cousins. Great memories are being made out in the country as my girls get to fish and hunt for frogs down by the creek.

My mother in-law also lives near us, so we see her quite often as well. The girls enjoy baking and playing board games at her house and especially love it when their cousins are visiting. Even during the pandemic, we have chosen to gather with our family. We are aware of the risk, especially with me being a healthcare provider potentially being exposed on the regular, but ultimately, we have decided that seeing our family is more important than any fears we might have. Thankfully, we've all stayed well. I know some families haven't been as lucky.

It saddens me when I hear of many families that haven't seen each other since this whole thing got started; people who have barely left their house in over 6 long months, people who haven't gotten to physically see or hug their grandchildren, and patients of mine who are so incredibly lonely. Some are sadly widowed and live alone and feel like they literally have no one. Sometimes their trip to the doctor's office is their only outing with people in months. Their visit with me turns into more of a social visit than anything else. They talk and I listen. And before Covid-19, we'd hug or shake hands.

One of the saddest parts of the global pandemic has been the social distancing and isolation that it has caused, as well as the lack of physical contact with others. People who live in assistant living or nursing homes haven't been able to see their family in months due to visitor restrictions. Even hospitals have restricted visitors, forcing people to sometimes die alone. Other people have chosen to isolate themselves out of fear of getting the virus. They haven't met their new grandbaby. They didn't get to attend their son or daughter's wedding. They've missed birthdays and holidays and special occasions all because of this virus.

Fill up to Spill out

Michael J. Fox has been quoted as saying "family is not an important thing. It's everything." Covid-19 is trying to take away community, but I am personally not going to let it rob me of time with my family or friends who are like my family. Life is what you make it, and I think it's so much better with family and friends even if gathering with them during this season is a bit of a risk.

Community is important. Whether we find community within our own family, our close-knit group of friends, our neighbors, or our coworkers, having people to connect with on a regular basis is so good for filling our cup. We were not created to do life alone. We were made for so much more.

More talking and listening.
More eating and drinking.
More hugging and embracing.
More smiling and laughing.
More sharing and giving.
More loving and comforting.

Do you find yourself craving community, but are having a hard time finding it? Do you not live near family, or maybe you just aren't that connected to them? I would encourage you to get plugged in at the places where you are bound to meet some new friends. Church is a great place to start, or at least when church is back to normal. Join a small group, volunteer in the nursery or be a greeter at the front door. Also seek out ways to get involved in your community. Look for common interest groups like a running club, group fitness, service groups, gardening clubs, book clubs, or crafting meetups. One friend often turns into a group of friends as that one friend introduces you to her other friends.

That's what happened with our big group of friends. It all started with one mutual friend who then introduced us to some of his friends, who brought their friends. And then we brought our friends from college. And we all became this amazing group of friends. That's how community starts. It all starts with one friend, and that one friend can be you.

Be that person that creates community. Be the woman that cheers on other women and looks for opportunities to be a good friend. Show up with the bottle of champagne or wine to celebrate another person's success or send a greeting card in the mail with kind words of encouragement as they go through a difficult time. Be the friend that shows up with a plant or a casserole as someone mourns the loss of a family member. Just show up.

My mom has always done this better than anyone I know, and my grandma did it too. If someone was hurting, they showed up with food. If someone needed help, they showed up ready to work. And we can show up too.

We are here on this Earth to love on other people. We are made to do life with one another, to build and strengthen our community. God created people to enjoy His beautiful creation, and He sent Jesus to show us how to love one another. He did not intend for us to do life alone or to be divided, but to do life with each other. We need people in our lives. We need to fill our cups with community.

Chapter 4

Fill up with fun

"Do anything, but let it produce joy."
Walt Whitman

Disney World is known as the happiest place on Earth, and if you've been there a time or two then you most certainly know why. From all the different parks, unique dining experiences, abundance of characters, exciting shows and rides, and impeccable service, to the amazing display of fireworks over Cinderella's castle each night, there is nothing quite like it. It is so much fun. We've been blessed to be able to take our girls there twice in the last 5 years, and both times were completely magical. I would go there every year if it wasn't so darn expensive. But it's pricey for a reason. It takes a lot of people to produce that level of joy, and I think it's worth every penny.

The good news is, we don't have to go to Disney World every year to experience fun and excitement in our lives (although I wouldn't object). In fact, we can create it right in our backyard. It just requires being intentional about creating opportunities for fun.

In our world of busy, busy, busy, we sometimes forget what it's like to really have fun. We get so wrapped up in work and responsibilities that we simply fail to schedule fun things. Instead our calendars are filled with work, meetings, monotonous tasks and responsibilities, and all our kid's activities. Sometimes it takes going to Disney World, riding roller coasters all day while sipping on frozen lemonades and eating Mickey Mouse shaped pretzels to remember that life can be pretty fun if we make it that way.

Kids aren't the only ones who need to have fun. We all benefit from incorporating fun into our everyday lives. Our cups run dry when all we are doing is working and taking care of everyone and everything. Just like we schedule fun things for our kids to do like recreational sports and extra-curricular activities, play-dates and birthday parties, we need to create pockets of fun for us too. Fun things produce joy in our lives and filling our cup with more joy definitely results in a ripple effect to those around us. Tired, grumpy, stressed-out mom doesn't benefit anyone, but fun, happy, joy-filled mom adjusts the thermostat of the entire house. Don't you agree? When mom's happy, everyone's happy (and the same thing goes for dad).

When we were kids, our lives revolved around having fun. We'd play with our friends in the backyard for hours, jumping on the trampoline and running through the water sprinkler. We'd ride our bikes and stop to buy a favorite cold treat from the ice-cream truck, and then we'd go play some more. We were carefree, and life was fun. Even in college and our years before having kids of our own, we would make time for fun. We'd camp at the lake and roast marshmallows over the open fire, float the river with friends and a big cooler of drinks, go on date nights with dinner and a movie, play put-put golf or go bowling, enjoy tropical summer trips with friends, but most importantly, we made time for fun.

When was the last time you did something that was all about having fun? Did it bring you immense joy? Did it take you back to those years of being a kid again? Did it fill you up like nothing else? Did you laugh and smile and go to bed with a full heart?

I'll admit that I can be a pretty serious person sometimes. I get wrapped up in work and responsibilities and personal goals of mine that I sometimes forget to just laugh and have fun. Kids aren't the only ones who need play in their lives, but grown-ups also need to play and be filled up. George Bernard Shaw says that "we don't stop playing because we grow old; we grow old because we stop playing."

Fun things don't just happen, especially when you're a parent to small children. You have to plan them and be intentional about setting aside time to do things that are fun. If you want to have date night with your spouse or a girl's nights with your friends, you have to plan for it and arrange for childcare if needed. If you want to go on a trip or a fun little getaway, that will also require planning and preparation. Just like kids enjoy having something to look forward to, adults need to experience anticipation as well. I love looking at my calendar, counting down the weeks and days to something fun like a girls' night with my friends, a weekend getaway with the hubby, or big family vacation.

Many years ago, our group of friends started an annual tradition of going to the beach every summer. I think it started with about 8 or 9 families, but 5 families have continued going every single year. Our kids were babies when we started going to the beach together. And 11 years later, we are still planning this LTD summer beach trip and looking forward to it every single summer. You know what makes this trip so memorable and fun? It's not necessarily where we go or what kind of house we stay in, although we've stayed in some pretty amazing places. It's the fun we have together for those 4 days we're there. There's absolutely no better way to bond as friends than spending several nights together in one big house, waking up and cooking breakfast together, going for runs on the beach with friends, building sandcastles with one another, and staying up late talking and playing games. We don't just look forward to it every year, but our kids look forward to it as well. This trip requires planning and saving, coordinating of schedules and arrangements for our pets, but we always make it happen (even in the middle of a pandemic), and we hope to continue this tradition for many years to come.

We've also gone on a couple of ski trips with another group of friends. Like many of you, I could share all sorts of great stories from our ski adventures, especially our New Year's trip to Santa Fe, New Mexico. Some trips with friends make the best memories and that was definitely one of them with our flooded house and broken bed. But at least we got our puzzle put together!

I love my friends and they definitely make life more fun. When I am not getting together regularly with my friends, especially my girlfriends, my cup starts to run dry. I need my friends in my life. I need fun girl's nights to drink wine or margaritas, to laugh about motherhood or to have deep conversations about life's ups and downs. As life has gotten busier with kid's activities plus all of our crazy jobs and our husbands' busy schedules, making time for our friends has definitely become a bit more challenging. But we continue to make it a priority to gather every month or so. And when we're not getting together, we have a running group text message to check in on one another, send funny memes and videos back and forth, and to simply just be there for each other. Sometimes we need a good laugh, and sometimes we need big prayers. Having friends definitely lightens the load and makes life more joyful.

Creative outlets also add fun and joy to our lives. I'm not a super crafty person, but I do love writing, taking pretty photos and displaying them in creative ways, and I absolutely love decorating our home. Taking time to pursue my creative outlet probably fills my cup like nothing else. It's relaxing and restorative; it brings me peace and joy and also gives me a different kind of purpose.

My daughters and I enjoy painting pottery together at our favorite local art place. Not only is it fun, but it's peaceful and relaxing. We also like to organize things around the house. I realize that a lot of people don't find cleaning and organizing fun, but I actually really enjoy it, and I'm trying to raise girls who know how to take care of a home. It brings me great satisfaction and joy to make something look neat, clean, and pleasing to the eye. We geek out over watching all the home improvement shows about remodeling, editing, and decorating homes. They give us ideas on what to do with our own space, and it's fun.

Everyone needs a hobby or two that they love and enjoy. And no, work it not a hobby, even if my dad thinks it is. Hobbies are things you do when you are not at work. They are things that bring you joy and excitement, peace and calm, happiness and fun, and a bit of an escape from your everyday work life. Your hobby might be running or biking, photographing nature, reading books, playing tennis or golf, cooking or baking, traveling, attending Broadway musicals (oh, how I am missing those due to Covid), playing the piano, or shopping for antiques. You might enjoy going hunting or fishing. Running half marathons or doing triathlons might be the thing that lights your heart on fire. Or maybe your goal is to see all 50 states, so planning each trip is your jam. Maybe you love camping out in the great outdoors, kayaking and hiking, and just enjoying nature. Whatever your passion is, it is unique to you, and it's something that truly brings you joy. It's fun, and we need more fun in our lives.

Covid-19 has hugely affected the way we have fun, especially if our idea of fun was wrapped up in entertainment and live events. All our plans, activities, and much anticipated events have been sadly cancelled. Weddings, vacations, concerts, sporting events, musicals, field trips, prom, graduation, marathons, book tours, and fun birthday parties are all being cancelled or postponed indefinitely. Cruise ships have been docked. Flights have been cancelled. Filming for shows and movies has ceased. It's crazy how quickly everything can change, how something like a virus can come in and wipe out the travel and entertainment industry in a matter of days.

My parents love going on cruise ships. They enjoy getting away but prefer to have everything planned out for them. They like to watch concerts and comedy shows, play black-jack and the slot machines, and they enjoy not having to cook or clean for a week. They get away so they can rest and escape. This pandemic has stollen this primary source of fun and entertainment from them and millions of other cruise-lovers. It's still unclear when cruise ships will be allowed to cruise again, leaving my parents feeling restless and bored at times. Like a lot of other people, this time has been challenging for them. It's forced my parents and others to have to think outside the box, to come up with new and creative ways of having fun and exploring while remaining safe.

My mother in-law enjoys being around people. Unlike me, she's definitely more of an extrovert and thrives around people and getting to go all over the state with her friends. She is part of an organization that meets regularly and requires a lot of driving. Covid-19 has forced their group to put things on hold for a while. Her car has never sat still this long. She has never had to be at home this much, feeling isolated from her friends and former life before all this social distancing. She too has had to adjust to the current state of our world, finding joy in different things besides social events and travel.

Due to an unfortunate turn of events, our military family that we were supposed to visit in Germany ended up catching one of the last flights back to Texas before international travel came to a screeching halt due to the pandemic. A change of assignment landed them at a base just a couple of hours away from us for the year, allowing us to spend 2020 together. What a blessing for our kids to have each other during such a strange year; time for fishing and outdoor adventures, holidays spent together, and time for old fashioned fun out at the land of their future forever home.

This season of change and uncertainty is definitely teaching us how to search for joy and create fun even in times of darkness. When the lights are turned off at stadiums, museums, movie theaters, shopping malls and even Disneyworld, we're learning how to get creative in our homes. We're going back to simple forms of entertainment like building forts, playing board games, going on walks in the neighborhood, planting gardens, reading books, painting, and writing letters to friends. Things like flour and yeast, puzzles and bikes are sold out everywhere as people are turning to baking, biking, and putting puzzles together with their family. Quiet days have led to simple pleasures. We are reminded that we can still have fun, laugh and smile even while life as we know it takes a little pause.

Fill up to Spill out

As the months go by, I keep asking the same question. What is it that God is trying to teach us through Coronavirus and all the change surrounding this pandemic? I can come up with all sorts of answers, but more than anything, I think He's teaching us to slow down in order to be present with the people we love and to appreciate the little things in life. We thrive on busy. We think that in being busy and filling our calendars with all sort of plans we are creating purpose and joy. But sometimes all those plans don't equal fun and joy. Sometimes all they end up causing is stress.

Coronavirus is forcing us to slow down, reevaluate what truly matters, and just be still. Some of us need to learn how to put our phones down, be present with our kids, and find ways to create simple fun for our family. Some of us need to be reminded that it's important to play and have fun and connect with those we love. We can still find little joys and pleasure all around us if we look. God is teaching us to be inventive and creative. We are having to change a lot of the ways we do things including the way we stay entertained. He is also teaching us about gratitude. We will all have a new sense of appreciation for the things we often took for granted like being able to go to school, enjoy community, eat at local restaurants, watch sports, go to the movies, work out at the gym, go to the spa, go on vacation, and all the things that make up the life we love.

If you were someone that didn't really prioritize fun before this pandemic, then life isn't really much different for you right now, besides maybe the challenge of finding toilet paper. You wonder what everyone is so sad about. You wonder why people are mourning the life they had before Covid. You don't understand why someone is grieving the loss of vacations, 5K runs, musicals, art classes, girl's trips, sporting events, and other fun things. You are used to staying home. You are used to working 24/7, not using your vacation days or making time to have some fun.

I have actually had patients tell me this as I have asked them how they are coping with all the change and disappointment surrounding Covid. Surprisingly some don't feel like their current life during this pandemic is any different than before. They spend most of their days working and little time playing. Or they're retired and just spend all their time at home. They've never flown on an airplane nor have they gone to a live music concert, and they actually prefer to socially distance themselves from people and public places. How sad.

I hope this is not you. I hope that you don't spend all of your time working or sitting at home, never allowing yourself to have any fun. We need to take time to fill our cup with fun things. We need to go places and experience life in different ways. Our ideas of fun might be different, but we all feel better and therefore give better when we are making time for play. I encourage you to work hard but play hard too. The best memories are made when we are having fun. Take time to enjoy the good life, play with your kids or grandkids, gather with friends, plan trips, have date nights, be creative, explore nature and its beauty, read a good book on the patio, be part of a community, and just laugh more, smile more, and fill your cup with plenty of joy.

Chapter 5

Fill up with rest

"Rest and self-care are so important. When you take time to replenish your spirit, it allows you to serve others from the overflow. You cannot pour from an empty vessel."

Eleanor Brownn

I hate taking naps. As a toddler, I fought naps with everything I had. I didn't want to miss out on anything, so the thought of sleeping during the day simply felt like a waste of time, and I wanted *all* of my hours. Even when I had babies of my own and struggled to keep my eyes open after a sleepless night with a crying baby, I refused to take a nap. People told me to sleep when the baby sleeps, even during the day, but I felt like I needed to be doing something productive during that hour, so instead I drank a Diet Coke while folding laundry or washing bottles. A sleeping baby meant I had time to actually get things done, so I hustled while she slept. Maybe it wasn't the best thing to do, but I knew I wouldn't get to take naps when I went back to work. So instead, I forced my body to get used to surviving on less sleep until each baby started sleeping through the night. Even to this day, I refuse to take naps or sleep in, as I am writing this chapter in the early morning hours while the rest of my house sleeps. But although I don't take naps or enjoy sleeping in on the weekends, I do make time for rest.

Just like we need to make time for fun, we also need to invest in time to rest and renew. In our season of working and raising kids, we tend to go fast and furious all the time. We have work, kids, and endless chores and responsibilities. Our evenings are even filled with activities as we taxi our kids around town. All this stuff on our plate starts to feel heavy after a while. If we are not intentional about our sleep and setting aside time for rest, we can only go so long. We eventually have to fill up that tank, and what we often need isn't another Diet Coke, but some rest.

The first step in creating time for rest is learning to say no. I've said it before, and I'll say it again. We can't do all things or be all things to all people. Got it? We need time to ourselves, and we need time to rest. This means saying yes to what's important and necessary and no to everyone and everything else. Claudia Black says that "saying no can be the ultimate self-care."

Each time you say yes, committing to one more thing, you are saying no to your opportunity for rest. When you say yes, you are choosing someone else's agenda over your own needs and desires. You're saying yes to what's important to them and not necessarily what's important to you. I'm not telling you to always say no, because there are definitely things in life we need to say yes to. Yes, to loving and serving when it's an important cause to you. Yes, to helping a neighbor that always helps you. Yes, to a family member or friend when they need your presence and listening ear. Yes, to the things that bring you peace, joy, and purpose.

But say no to the things that take all your time and energy, leaving you with none for yourself or your family. Say no to the things that aren't important to you. Say no to the people that bring you down or stress you out. Say no to the things that don't bring you peace, joy, or purpose. Say no to the things that you just don't have time to do. Learn to politely say no. Learn to prioritize what truly matters. Learn to respect your own time and energy, realizing that time for rest and protecting your peace is super important.

I've gotten really good at saying no over the last several years. As a working mom I don't have a lot of extra time. I respect the time that I do have so that I can be present for my girls and my husband and show up well for the things that I love. I help and volunteer where I can, while also saying no to commitments that I know I don't have time for. I pick and choose what's important, what brings me or my family peace, joy, or purpose. Jen Hatmaker says "There are only 24 hours in a day. We need to quit trying to be awesome and instead be wise." I've learned to be wise with my time and how I use it. And sometimes I just need days with no agenda or commitments. I just need rest and you do too.

As we walk through Coronavirus and our lives continue to be turned upside down, one of the positive things that has come out of this is all the extra time we have gained as everything has been cancelled. Some of us are still going to work to do essential jobs, learning how to do things differently and trying not to take the virus home to our families. Others are being forced to stay home, some with kids, others alone. One thing that most of us are experiencing is more time.

Our evenings are quiet, as we are not rushing off to our kid's activities. There are no sports on TV to watch. All forms of entertainment and gathering of people have been cancelled. We are not allowed to eat out at a restaurant. We can barely leave our house. As trapped as we all feel right now, we can't help but also feel free; free to take walks in the neighborhood, free to sit out on the patio and read a good book and watch our kids play, free to kick up our feet and watch a movie, free to go on a family bike ride on a cool spring night, free to talk on the phone the way that we used to not worried about the time, free to look through old photo albums and create new ones. This time is a gift. For a lot of us, it's time to rest and renew.

It's important to create these pockets of time for rest. We have to learn to intentionally leave blank spaces on our calendar to have a slower start to our day, make pancakes for the family, sit out on the patio with coffee and a good book, and just allow our bodies to rest. I love weekends where we have time to do this very thing. As much as I love gathering with friends, attending fun events, and watching our girls play their sports, sometimes what I am craving is just a Saturday with nothing to do but be home. We need quiet weekends every once in a while. Just like our family craves fun and excitement, we also crave rest.

Using our vacation time is so important. So many people fail to use their time off of work each year, because they feel guilty about being away. They actually lose those hours because they don't use them. How sad is that? We need to use our days, and not just for fun and adventure, home projects or kid's field trips, but for rest. Use your time to plan a relaxing, restful vacation. Plan a long weekend getaway to rest by a pool, get a massage, and sip on mimosas while reading a good book. Or take a week off to have a staycation. Stay at home and do things that bring you peace. We often don't spend enough time just being home, except for maybe right now during this global pandemic.

This last Christmas, we decided to just stay home during the time we both had off work. Normally, we might go on a ski trip with friends or go on a road trip to see family. But this year, we just stayed home, and it was absolutely wonderful. My husband was finally able to finish his dissertation for his doctoral degree while the girls and I had time to clean, organize, and simplify things around the house. I tackled closets and clothing drawers, as well as the pantry and all the things. We put away the Christmas decorations while giving the house a good cleaning. This may sound like work to some of you, but it was so incredibly relaxing and renewing for my spirit, especially the end result. We played dominoes at night, ate popcorn and watched movies, played old-school Nintendo, and just enjoyed some much-needed family time at home. My husband probably didn't find it as restful as we did but having that time to knock out his paper was definitely weight lifted off his shoulders. We went back to work and school feeling rested and renewed, ready to tackle a new year. It made me crave more time like that.

Sometimes we just need to stay home and enjoy the comfort of our environment and our family. Our homes are sacred, and often the way life is, we don't get to really enjoy the beautiful space we have created. I have certain spaces in my home that bring me so much joy. I adore my little coffee station where I start each day by pouring a hot cup of coffee and adding my favorite cinnamon creamer. I love my cozy "office" space (actually our formal dining room) where I do my early morning routine of journaling, reading, planning my day, and writing like I'm doing right now. I am surrounded by my unique cross collection, a wall filled with at least 50 crosses that I have collected over the years. The room has 2 large windows with good lighting and a great table with a hutch filled with all of our china, crystal, and some of my grandmother's cherished pieces. Our formal dining room is rarely used for dining but is one of my favorite rooms in the house. It is comfortable and filled with special pieces and the memories I associate with those pieces. I also love our back patio when it's nice enough to sit out there to enjoy the view of the back yard, the animals that often come up to our back fence, and the gorgeous sunrises.

Do you have some special rooms or spaces in your house that bring you joy? Spaces that you have thoughtfully created that help you rest and renew? Is it your spa-like bathroom, cozy family room with fluffy blankets and pillows, creative craft room, or maybe your front porch with your cute little rockers and potted plants? If you don't have a favorite spot, consider transforming different spaces in your home to allow for more joy, more peace, and more rest.

Or maybe the beach is actually where you prefer to be. The beach is definitely one of my happy places. I especially love going there during non-peak seasons like early spring or in the fall, when the temperatures aren't so hot, and the beaches are less crowded. I especially like not having to wear a bathing suit. I love walking the quiet beaches early in the morning as the sun is coming up and again in the evening as the sun is going down. There is nothing that makes me happier than hearing the crash of the waves, feeling the soft squishy sand between my toes, and watching the sun paint a heavenly picture across the wide-open sky. I feel at peace with an enormous sense of gratitude for life and everyone in it. I feel relaxed and restored.

One of our favorite trips to the beach was last year over spring break. We stayed at one of our favorite places, just our little family of four, along with our dog, and had the absolute best time just being together. We walked the clean, un-crowded beach, picked up interesting shells, let our dog run crazy as she chased after birds, flew kites, worked on a puzzle that notoriously ended up with one missing piece, read books while sipping our coffee, built sandcastles, and relaxed in the hot tub at night. It was fabulous. It was one of the most relaxing vacations we've ever experienced.

We have also enjoyed our trips to the mountains. Sunrises and sunsets at the beach are amazing, but in the mountains, they are absolutely majestic. The cool temperatures, the breath-taking views, all the different trees and vegetation, the sounds of nature, and the endless hiking trails are just some of the reasons we love the mountains. There's something so relaxing about waking up to those views, enjoying coffee and brunch at a cute little café in town, then hitting the trails to explore nature. I love getting to wear comfy shoes and stretchy pants all week, I love the slow pace and the friendly people, and I love taking pictures and making memories with my family. It doesn't get much better than that.

So, do I love the beach or the mountains more? That's a tough choice. I love both, and we actually got to enjoy both when we went to Lake Tahoe, California a few years ago with family. We got to play along the sandy shores of the beach while looking at the beautiful mountain landscape in front of us. The water was icy cold, but we still enjoyed playing in the sand, picnicking on the beach, and going on canoe rides with a stunning view. Talk about the best of both worlds. It was amazing. Sometimes you don't have to choose one or the other if you can find both in the same place. Score!

Whether you love relaxing at the sandy beach, the mountains, on a big cruise ship, at a luxurious spa resort, a cozy campsite, or even in the comfort of your own home, it's important to make time for vacations or staycations. We all need time to rest and renew. We need time to unplug and get away from our regular scheduled programing. We are so much better when we are taking breaks from everyday life, when we have to time to relax and focus on what truly matters.

Sometimes we are going so fast and pushing so hard that we don't stop and just look around and thank God for the beauty of life and our surroundings. We live in a truly magnificent world, and we need to make time to see it and truly appreciate it. I can't encourage you enough to get out and explore God's creation. Travel to different states. Go camping. Leave the country if you can. See new places, try different foods, run in different cities, relax on a beach with a good book and a cold beverage, explore different trails, go snorkeling in the ocean, or do some wine tasting in wine country (another favorite place of ours).

Whatever your idea of vacation is, just make time for it. You'll never regret the money you spent on traveling and spending time connecting with the people you love, but you'll definitely regret spending all your days on Earth just working or sitting at home. Are you working to make a living or working to make a life?

Fill your cup with rest. Take time for you and the things that restore you. Give yourself permission to just be still, relax, and breathe. Choose what brings you peace and joy, renews your spirit, calms your soul, and say no to the things that don't. Make time for rest and all its many benefits.

Allison R. Smith

Chapter 6

Fill up with personal growth

"If you want to truly be fulfilled, you need to be growing." Dave Hollis

Sometimes my patients like to jokingly ask me where I come from, as apparently my southern or country twang accent is even strong for this part of Texas. They expect me to say somewhere like Georgia or Alabama or maybe Kentucky. And instead, I respond with Texas, as in right here deep in the heart of Texas. I'm not sure why they act so shockingly surprised as a lot of us Texans have accents, but apparently mine sometimes stands out like a sore thumb. My strong southern accent and my youthful appearance are just two of the things my patients like to comment on as I interact with them during their visit.

"Surely, you're not old enough to be doing this."

"Wow, you're such a young pretty doctor (even though I just introduced myself as a family nurse practitioner, and I am indeed old enough to be a doctor if I had chosen the path to be one)!"

"You must not be from around her with that strong accent of yours. Where are you from?"

These comments used to bother me, and sometimes they still do, but I've also learned to just embrace who I am and who I am becoming. Yes, I look young for my age, often still getting carded at the grocery store at the age of nearly 41 (and hopefully I always will). And yes, I sometimes sound like a country bumpkin (after all, I grew up as a farmer's daughter, no offense to my parents). But it's who I am, and it's where I've come from, and I'm still growing into who I am becoming in this life of mine. I suppose it's better than being asked if I'm pregnant when I'm obviously not. I did have a patient once ask me that, and you better believe that shirt went straight into the donation pile as soon as I got home that night.

Like a lot of the great people I've gotten to know over the years, I too have lived in the same area of central Texas my entire life. It's a great place. What can I say? I live just over 30 miles from where I grew up, and my parents and siblings still live on the same country dirt roads I learned to drive on. Texas is home, and Texas is probably where I'll always be.

Additionally, I've worked for the same healthcare organization for over 18 years now, only changing job sites 3 times due to promotion or transfer. I've been at my current clinic for 10 years now, and I've grown to love the many generations of patients I get to care for. I'm not a huge fan of change. It's not that I'm completely opposed to change, as I know it allows for growth, but I just don't love big change. I don't like starting over when I've finally gotten comfortable. I like seeing new places and doing new things, but I also enjoy coming home to what's familiar and safe.

My husband has changed jobs many times over the years. He's worked in 4 different school districts, teaching and coaching at different grade levels and gradually working his way up the career ladder to his current role as principal. He's sat through countless interviews, met tons of new faces, and he's had to learn all sorts of new skills over the years as he's gone from first year teacher to principal. But I think he kinds of likes the challenge of a new job. He enjoys change, or at least he openly embraces it.

My husband's sister and her family live the military lifestyle that so many brave families choose to live. They move from one place to another every 1-3 years, packing up all of their household goods and relocating to a new Airforce base, sometimes overseas. This way of life forces them to say goodbye to friends and make new ones over and over again. The thought of doing that frightens me a little bit as I prefer familiar and safe, but they've learned to do it with such ease and resilience. They've sacrificed so much over the years, but I don't think they've ever looked at it that way, as they've always kept a great attitude even when certain moves have been hard. Even their kids have gotten used to moving from one school to the next, picking up and starting over again, learning to grow and adapt to constant change.

There is much to be learned from families that live the military lifestyle. Us civilians look at this way of life as difficult, stressful, potentially lonely, and even scary. But families that live it see adventure and opportunities to create their own sense of family, making new friends at each stop and relying on each other like they've known one another for years. They develop a sense of pride for their country and what they do and the uniform they wear, newfound strength within them, patience and flexibility, and incredible resilience. And of course, there's also the perks of benefits galore, military discounts, and early retirement. Military life isn't for everyone, but I am proud of my family members and others who choose to serve our country in this wonderful way.

Sometimes change is a choice that we make for ourselves like moving to a new town or state, leaving one job for another, or choosing to pursue a new hobby or goal, but often times change is something that is out of our control. With each season we go through, change is going to happen. And sometimes we don't like it. Change can be hard. Change can be scary.
We are experiencing a crazy enormous amount of change right now as we walk through the Covid-19 pandemic. In the last

several months our lives have been literally turned upside down. Schools across the country have been forced to close their doors, and parents are being encouraged to "home-school" their children with virtual instruction, even though it's somewhat impossible with parents who work. Businesses have closed, causing millions of people to lose jobs and their livelihood, standing in incredibly long lines to file for unemployment. Others are working from home, having to stressfully navigate both working remotely while also helping their kids with virtual school.

Those of us with "essential" jobs like healthcare workers, first responders, grocery workers, and others are feeling overwhelmed by the change and heaviness of it all. Nothing feels normal as we are required to wear a claustrophobic mask all day and have our temperature checked as we walk into the building to work. Things are uncertain, and with uncertainty comes all sorts of emotions. It's scary and different, we feel "trapped" and frustrated and even sad. We are all grieving a little bit (or maybe a lot) for the life we knew before Coronavirus. We aren't sure how long this season is going to last. We find ourselves pivoting to only have to pivot once again. We want things to be normal. We want to be able to go to work as usual, eat at a local restaurant, shop without fear, gather with friends and family, attend live events with crowds of people, and travel without restrictions.

Change is hard, but change can also be good if we choose to see it that way. We find comfort in things like stability and job security as well as our normal routines and habits. But we also have the incredible opportunity to learn and grow through change, discomfort, and a disruption of those routines and habits.

We are either going to grow in 2020, or we are going to miss out on the chance to come out stronger and wiser. We can thrive or just simply survive. The choice is ours. We can throw in the towel, sulk about the situation, complain and consume negative stuff and cope in negative ways, or we can get creative, learn new skills, consume positive content, establish better routines and habits, and choose to grow our minds while we have this extra time and opportunity.

I'll admit that my ability to thrive in this crazy season has gone through some ebbs and flows. I have definitely experienced days where I feel like I am just going through the motions at work and home and simply trying to survive this challenging time. I'm tired of wearing a mask at work, I want my kids to be back in school, I miss community and running in races, and I miss all of our many forms of entertainment. Some days I just don't feel like stretching or growing. I just don't feel that motivated or inspired to learn something new. I just want this to be over with. I want the news to stop talking about. I just want to wake up from this terrible dream to find out that it didn't actually happen and that everything is normal the way it used to be before Covid. Unfortunately, that never happens.

But I do pick myself back up and decide that thriving versus surviving is simply a choice I get to make each day, and I choose to grow and thrive. I fix my attitude and put forth the necessary effort to get back on track and start filling my cup with personal growth and development again. I intentionally choose to stay grounded in my already established routines and habits, and I try to motivate others to do the same.

Months into this global pandemic, I am still waking up early and doing my morning routine, choosing gratitude and pursuing the goals that are important to me. I am moving my body, still running and training for races that I will only get to run virtually. I am intentionally reading more books and consuming positive content through podcasts and inspiring pages on social media instead of watching the news, which feels negative and politically driven these days. I am learning new ways of doing things both at work and at home. I am choosing a growth mindset over a fixed mindset, and I am actively pursuing joy every single day. I don't just want to survive this season, but I want to thrive as we go through it.

Growing through life is a choice. Choosing to stay the same when everything around us is changing is also a choice. Just like a plant, we were made to grow. God created us to bloom, to not just grow up, but to rise up and flourish into the person He made us to be. None of us chose Covid-19. None of us asked for change and heartbreak and challenge in 2020, but like anything else that's come our way, we get to choose how we react and respond to this crisis and how we learn and grow through it all.

Are we taking advantage of the extra time we have? Are we documenting this historical year we are living through? Are we processing it and writing about it? Are we getting creative and pivoting in our jobs and in our small businesses? Are we learning anything from this new and different perspective on life? Are we loving like Jesus? Are we choosing gratitude, grace, and kindness when it seems like no one else is? Are we consuming the right content, listening to the right sources, and following the right kind of people?

We are what we consume. It's as simple as that. The things we feed our bodies either fuel us or weigh us down. In the same way that we feel bad when we eat bad, it's no surprise that our mental and emotional health is also affected by what we consume. When we surround ourselves with negative people and consume negative forms of media and content, we start to feel anxious, depressed and overwhelmed causing an unpleasant ripple effect to those around us. When we are consuming the same old thing every day, not learning and growing and improving, we also start to feel bored and unfulfilled.

But when we are consuming positive content and surrounding ourselves with positive people who are intentionally living with joy and purpose, we also start to grow and feel better, and the rewards spill out to those around us. We were created to grow and change, focus on the good around us, and make a positive impact on others. Personal growth is a lifelong journey with no finish line or destination. When we simply choose to stop learning and growing, part of us dies. And we still have a lot of living left to do.

So how do we keep growing our minds? What does personal growth really look like? What do we need to be doing to make sure we grow and thrive through life and all its curveballs?

Remember all the books you read when you were growing up? You just thought you were done reading when you graduated high school or college. One of the best ways to keep learning and growing is to keep reading. Readers are lifelong learners. We read books to learn more about the things we are interested in. We read to be inspired. We read to escape. We read to be motivated. We read more to know more. Maya Angelou says "Do the best you can until you know better. Then when you know better, do better." Reading is a great way to learn more so you can know more and do better after gaining new knowledge and a different perspective on life.

These days, I mostly read non-fiction, because I love books that guide me on this journey to becoming a better version of myself. I love getting inspired by reading about other people's lives and their wildly different experiences. Reading their stories gives me courage to share my own story but also pursue things I'm interested in. I occasionally throw in a fiction book, because sometimes we need to just escape to another place, get wrapped up in different characters, and be inspired by different adventures. But whether we read fiction or non-fiction, reading is good for growing our minds. Leaders are readers, so if we want to lead well at home, work, or in our community, we need to be reading.

Do you not feel like you have time to sit down and physically read a book? You're not alone. Try listening to audiobooks. I love listening to authors narrate their own books. They truly bring their book to life as you can hear their heart as they read their words to you. Listening to an audiobook on your commute, your runs, your evening walks with the dog, or while doing chores around the house is a great way to multi-task and consume more books. It's how I've been able to add so many more books to my life. I can usually only read one physical book a month (or maybe more when we're on vacation), but I listen to several more while doing other things. Sometimes I even prefer this way of reading as I feel like I can connect with the author and their story even more.

Speaking of listening to books, podcasts are another great way to grow your mind. For those of you who aren't familiar, podcasts are free recorded talk shows that you can listen to from any of your devices. You can probably find a podcast about literally anything you are interested in. Most authors, speakers, athletes, and influencers have a podcast these days. You can listen to inspiring interviews, learn how to train your dog, be encouraged by a Christian leader, or just be entertained. I absolutely love podcasts and listen to them in the car, on walks, when I'm getting ready in the morning, and while I'm watching soccer practice. It's a nice change from just listening to music. Search your favorite author, speaker, or leader and I bet they have a podcast you'll love.

Attending trainings or conferences can also be a great tool to keep growing. In order to keep my professional license, I'm required to have continuing education hours each year. I attend medical conferences and trainings to learn about changes and gain new knowledge and recommendations that I can take back to my practice. Other professions require this as well. But have you ever thought about going to a personal growth conference to gain knowledge about how to live your best life? I've attended a few of these over the years, and I can tell you that they were my favorite. Hearing experts speak with such passion on topics like nutrition, fitness, faith, and overall physical and mental wellness was extremely motivational and helpful in my health and personal growth journey. And in this time of Covid-19, a lot of these conferences have gone virtual, making it easy to view the content in the comfort of your own home. If you're finding yourself feeling less motivated, consider investing in a course or training that will inspire you to grow physically, mentally, or spiritually.

In the digital age we now live in, we have no excuse for not growing. Want to learn how to change a flat tire? I bet you can find thousands of YouTube videos that will show you step by step how to do it. Want to be better at cooking or baking? You can search literally a million recipes using your google search bar. Between social media, YouTube, Pinterest, and other platforms, you can figure out how to do almost anything these days. All it takes is a willingness to learn, practice, and get better.

Choosing to stay stuck or stagnant is a choice. Want to learn more? Seek out educational opportunities to do so. Go back to school, take an online course, attend a training, read more books, listen to more podcasts, learn from others who are ahead of you, and choose to view change as an opportunity to grow.

Max DePree says, "We cannot become what we want to be by remaining what we are." We must keep growing, filling our cup with knowledge, skills, and motivational fuel to keep going. We don't stay fulfilled by doing the same things every day. We grow through change. We grow through life's experiences. We grow by educating ourselves and learning new skills. We grow by being challenged. We grow through our discomfort and fears, choosing to keep showing up even when it's hard.

This season is an opportunity for growth and resilience. We can either resist change, be angry about it and do nothing but simply whine and complain, or we can choose to pivot, gain new knowledge and perspective, learn new ways of doing things, and choose to grow. In order to live a life of purpose, we need to be filling our cups with personal growth.

Allison R. Smith

Chapter 7

Fill up with courage

"Each time we face our fear, we gain strength, courage, and confidence in the doing."
Theodore Roosevelt

At the beginning of 2020, I chose COURAGE as my word for the year. How appropriate, right? "Choose courage, make a greater impact" was my motto as I went into 2020 with anticipation and excitement. My goal was to choose courage as I put my first book out into the world, telling my story and sharing all my embarrassing vulnerabilities with those who would read it and possibly critique it. Initially the book was written for my girls and my close family members, but somewhere along the journey of writing it, I decided to self-publish my first book, making it available to the world. Writing had become my passion and my therapy, and suddenly I wanted to start encouraging more people with my written words. I needed courage to begin sharing more on social media, writing and blogging, creating my brand, and pursuing this new dream of mine as a writer and author. I didn't choose the word confidence, because historically it's what I have always struggled with, but instead I chose the word courage, because courage is what you need to gain confidence. I needed courage to start and courage to keep going.

What I didn't know is that I would also need courage when I was called back in after my very first mammogram, resulting in a full biopsy and anxious days of waiting for the results (which were thankfully benign). I also didn't know that I would need courage to keep showing up as a health care provider in the middle of a global pandemic. Did anyone else plan for that? I certainly didn't as I was planning out my year and writing out my goals and visions for 2020. But I sure am glad I chose the word, courage, because courage is what would end up getting me through this absolutely crazy year.

Historically, when it has come to my big goals, I've always been someone that fully commits and stays the course until I achieve them. I'm not a quitter (except for that one time in high school), and neither is my husband. We dream big, choose ambitious goals for ourselves, and we do the work that is needed to achieve them. It's just the way we are, and I love this about us. We've pushed ourselves to run three marathons, go back to school, further our careers, invest our money wisely, and we're actively striving to travel to all 50 states with our kids. We don't just say we're going to do something and later flake out, but we go all-in and pursue it until it's done. We choose things that are difficult. We do things that others don't want to do or don't think they can do. We challenge ourselves to be better. It's definitely not confidence that pushes us to do these things we've never done before, so what is it?

It's COURAGE.

Do you know people that are always announcing new goals, sharing their journey on social media for a few weeks, and then suddenly they don't mention it anymore, and then they've moved on to something else that they will also quit in a few weeks? I am not that person, but a lot of people are. They start and stop and never finish anything they've begun. They try all the latest diets, they announce that they are training for a half marathon but never end up running it, they express their interest in going back to school but never commit, or they say they're going to write a book and never get past the first chapter. By never completing anything they start, they miss out on the confidence that is gained by pushing past the discomfort, having the courage to stay the course, and ultimately achieving their goal.

Having the courage to ultimately finish what we've started results in confidence. Each time that we conquer a big fear or accomplish a hard thing, we gain confidence. We don't just have confidence, but we earn it by choosing courage. Fear keeps us stuck, but courage leads us to unbelievable joy and confidence.

It's definitely something I've had to learn over the years. As someone who has historically struggled with confidence, putting myself out there has always been difficult for me. I absolutely hate public speaking or anything else that draws attention to me. It's not that I don't have ambition or dedication, but rather lack of confidence to be in the spotlight. Most of my big goals have been achieved away from the spotlight. I've run 3 marathons, but my husband and kids have been the only ones who have seen me run them. I mostly trained alone and ended up running 2 of them alone (Ted and I ran my first one together). My books have also been written and edited alone. When I've hit the publish button, I am the only one who has read them or touched them.

See, I can do hard things, as long as I'm not in the spotlight. Being in the spotlight, doing something like public speaking, is what causes me to ask a million questions.

What will others think about me? What if I mess up? What if I'm not good enough? What if no one likes like what I say? What if they think I sound like a country bumpkin from Alabama? What if no one supports my dream? What if no one buys my books? What if? What if?

These are valid questions and concerns, and I'm sure that a lot of you have also asked them, but they all have to do with a lack of confidence. And it's not confidence that we need to get started, but rather courage. Because the only way to gain confidence is choosing courage over fear. Each act of courage builds more confidence. Each time we finish what we've started we gain momentum to keep chasing that goal. We shouldn't let a lack of confidence hold us back from taking the first step to do something hard and definitely shouldn't let it stop us from finishing what we've started. It's not confidence that we need in our tanks, but rather courage.

And now that I understand that it's courage that I need, it's made all the difference in the world. Am I speaking on stages in front of people? Not yet. But am I standing up for myself, speaking out when I feel it's important, and putting myself out there more and more? Absolutely.

Do you think that a baby learning to walk feels confident when they take that first wobbly step while still holding on to something for a little support? No. But with courage and practice, one step turns into two steps and pretty soon they are walking all the way across the room, as their parents cheer and try to capture it on video. Those first courageous steps lead to confidence.

Do you think when I signed up to run my first marathon, I felt confident that I would be able to run all 26.2 miles without dying? No! I wasn't even sure if I could run more than 13.1, as I had only run half marathons prior to signing up for a full. But with the proper training and an insane amount of courage, I painfully put one step in front of another for over 5 hours until I reached the finish line.

And you know what? I gained tremendous confidence. After that first marathon, I knew I could do anything I wanted to do with the right amount of courage and dedication. When I signed up for two more marathons in the following years, because one was apparently not enough, I didn't doubt that I would finish. I knew I could do it, because I had already proven to myself that I could do it and not die. So, I signed up, did the work to prepare my body, and when it came to race day those next two times, I finished what I set out to do. I knew it would be hard, I knew I would need loads of courage and determination, but I was also fairly confident that I would cross that finish line, because I had already proven to myself that I could do it. Courage as well as confidence gained from previous experience is what fueled me to run another 26.2 miles in about 6 hours.

So many incredible goals and exciting opportunities are within our reach with the right amount of courage. We don't need confidence; we simply need courage. Bob Goff loves to use this quote from the movie, We Bought a Zoo, "You know, sometimes all you need is twenty seconds of insane courage. Just literally twenty seconds of just embarrassing bravery. And I promise you, something great will come of it." He's right! Think of all the ideas you have in a day and how you quickly dismiss them because you lack the confidence you think you need to do them.

What if instead you chose to act on them with just 20 seconds of insane courage? Do you think you would realize that it's not confidence that you need, but rather courage?

Courage to say yes.

Courage to commit and come up with a good plan.

Courage to try and fail and get back up and keep going.

Courage to actually finish what you've started.

It's at the starting line that you need courage, and it's at the finish line that you gain confidence.

What are you starting and stopping right now? What is holding you back from pursuing the dreams of your heart? What keeps stopping you as you get started? What do you need to put into your tank to keep your engine going? What's going to give you the fuel you need to keep showing up even when it's hard? What's going to get you to the starting line and push you to the finish line? The answer is courage. You need courage to start, courage to keep going, and courage to finish the race.

If you're striving to live your best life as your very best self, you need to be filling your cup with buckets of courage. Have courage to walk through open doors, chase your dreams, and be the person God made you to be. Don't worry about what anyone else thinks. Don't doubt your ability. Don't stop when it gets hard. Don't compare yourself to others. Don't worry about how you'll finish. Just get started. Just keep going. Run your own race in your own lane at your own pace. Stay the course no matter what. Keep pushing. Keep learning and growing. And don't stop until you've reached the finish line.

Start by doing little things every single day that require courage. Start small, and then go bigger. If your goal is something like running a marathon, start by going on a walk every day with your dog. Then start training for a 5K race using an APP that builds you up from walking to running. Run the 5K and realize that you did it and it wasn't so bad, so sign up for another one. Then finish that one even faster and sign up for a 10K. Run a few of those and again see that you didn't die, and then push yourself to complete a half marathon. Do the work to train and have the courage to show up on race day. Run the 13.1 miles and get to the finish line without dying and decide to dream bigger. Sign up for the marathon in 6 months. Run, train, push yourself beyond discomfort, and show up with 20 seconds of insane courage at the starting line. Turn on your music and put one foot in front of the other for 26.2 painful miles and finally reach the finish line with tired feet but a full heart with confidence to last a lifetime.

In finishing something like a marathon, you not only realize that you can run for hours without dying, but you can also do other hard things in life. You realize that the only thing standing in your way of the finish line is the courage to start and not stop.

Courage is what you need more than anything else, and courage is what other people need to witness. Courage is contagious.

Seeing my husband run a marathon before me is what gave me the courage to run one myself. I didn't think I would ever be able to run for 5 or 6 hours without stopping but seeing him do it allowed me to see myself doing it too. If he could do it, then surely, I could figure out how to do it as well.

Do you ever feel like that? You don't think there is any way you could ever write a book or start your own business or purchase your first home, but then you see someone else going before you and doing the thing you dream about and realize that maybe you can do it too. We need to have courage to do big things so that others have courage to do them too. Our kids are watching, our friends are watching, and our peers are watching too. Each time we act with courage, we are planting seeds of courage in other people too. Jen Hatmaker says, "brave moms raise brave kids." I couldn't agree more.

To encourage is to instill courage, and my husband and I are intentionally encouraging our girls to be independent, authentic, creative, and kind. My girls frequently tell me about their great big ideas and aspirations, and I see courage in them as they pursue them. They are bravely showing up as their authentic selves, and I absolutely love it. Our oldest daughter wants to be a Texas Game Warden. She loves fishing, hunting, animals, and all things outdoors. Our youngest wants to be a performer. She loves music and dance and bending her body in ways that don't seem humanly possible. Each of our girls are embracing who God made them to be while being confident in who they are becoming. I like to think that we are raising brave girls because they see me and their dad choosing courage over fear. They see us going after big audacious goals and finishing them. What type of behavior are you modeling to your kids?

As Covid-19 was entering our country and starting to change everything around us, my family was spending a few days exploring Arizona over spring break. What was initially supposed to be a work trip ended up being a vacation as all work-related travel at my company was suddenly suspended. With non-refundable flights already purchased, we made the decision to go ahead and go even though my conference was cancelled. It's a trip we'll never forget, as the rest of the country was preparing for a pandemic, panic-buying and hoarding, we were just living the dream in God's country. We enjoyed seeing the majestic views of the Grand Canyon with cold snow falling all around us, and then we spent the following day hiking and exploring the beautiful town of Sedona.

There is a well-known trail with the largest natural sandstone arch in the area known as the Devil's Bridge. It's about a 4-mile round-trip hike with breathtaking views and natural rock staircases that take you up to the bridge. It is there that you can choose to bravely walk out onto the thin archway known as the Devil's Bridge while your family members stand across from you taking the infamous pictures. It definitely appears much scarier than it really is. From the spot where people stand with their phones or cameras, it looks as though your family member could easily fall to their death right there in front of you. I'm not even joking. But in actuality, it's relatively safe as long as you don't do something dumb. We saw plenty of that.

As someone that gets easily frightened by heights and even more scared by watching my kids do things that seem risky, it took some insane courage on my part to walk out onto the bridge with my girls that day. Us girls went first, followed by my husband who walked out there alone. We captured the memory with some cool photos, and more importantly we left that trip with more courage than before. I was brave that day. And in being brave, I showed my girls that they too can be brave (not that my fearless girls really needed me to show them). We are not just raising kids. We are shaping their minds and building their courage each day we're with them.

What courageous actions are you taking right now that are paving the way for others to also be brave? Who is watching you? Who is being inspired by your courage and action to also take big steps towards something that makes them nervous? Do you need to be brave so that in seeing you be brave your kids will also choose courage?

Several months into the pandemic, after many of our plans were changed, we decided to go see the Dakotas. On our mission to see all 50 states, we couldn't let something like Coronavirus keep us from traveling. So, we put on our masks, took all the appropriate precautions, and flew to an area of the country where the Covid numbers were low and most activities were outside. We explored the hidden gem of Medora, North Dakota getting a hefty dose of Christian American patriotism, then we went down and spent a few days seeing Mount Rushmore and all the beautiful places around it.

The girls had the opportunity to zip-line and do other fun outdoor activities. As I watched my 9 and 11 year-old girls walk up to the zip-line podium alone, and then proceed to get suited up and bravely propel across the long cable, I couldn't help but think that if they continue to have courage like they did that day, then nothing can stop them from pursuing their dreams. We don't need to raise our kids to be confident. We need to raise our kids to have courage (and be kind).

Not only did we do a little traveling during Coronavirus, but we also chose to send our girls to camp. Okay, now you're probably thinking we're crazy. We had signed up for this camp way before Covid-19 came into our lives and assumed that the pandemic would end up cancelling these plans like everything else. But much to our surprise, it didn't. Camp continued as planned, but with new safety measures in place. 10 weeks went by and the camp continued to do very well with the Covid situation. So, whether people thought we were crazy or not, we chose to go ahead and send the girls to their very first 1-week camp at the end of the summer.

They bravely went to camp not knowing a single person there and came home gaining new friends and a week full of fun memories. Were they a little nervous about going to a place with new people, masks, change, and uncertainty? Yes. Were we as parents worried about their ability to adapt and grow? A little. But we also knew that camp was something they really needed in a year filled with disappointment. They needed to find courage to overcome fears, choose kindness in making new friends, and grow in their walk with Christ. Camp did all of those things for our girls, who came home excited about going back next year (when hopefully things are normal again).

What I've learned by being a parent for 11 years is that we need to put our kids into uncomfortable situations. We need to let them figure some things out on their own; to meet new people and take a few risks, to discern what's safe and what's not. It's good for them. When we make everything easy for our kids, always protecting them and holding them back, they don't have opportunities to act courageously. We need to encourage our kids to learn and grow, be brave, and take action even when it's hard. They need to learn what it feels like to experience a little bit of fear, as well as failure and disappointment. Afterall, that's life, and it's through change, discomfort, and failure that we grow the most.

2020 is giving us plenty of opportunities to be brave as we are being challenged to choose courage over confidence, change over comfort, and purpose over fear. Nothing is the same, and everything keeps changing. Our routines have been disrupted, there is fear and anxiety all around us, and the future is filled with all sorts of uncertainty. But we are bravely learning how to adapt, adjusting to a life filled with wearing masks and social distancing. We are figuring out how to educate our children while keeping everyone safe. Decisions are difficult. Confidence is scarce. But courage is not. We are leaning on courage as we walk through this challenging season. Courage is what is allowing us to stay calm and carry on. Courage is going to get us to the finish line. So, as we think about what goes into our cups each day, we shouldn't focus on filling our cups with confidence, but instead filling them with overflowing buckets of courage.

Chapter 8

Fill up with goals

"The only real purpose of a goal is to inspire you to fall more deeply in love with life." Michael Neill

The definition of busy is having a great deal to do, and when I was a teenager, busy was my middle name. I grew up in a small town in Texas where it was common to play multiple sports, march in the band wearing a cheerleader outfit, and work at the local grocery store on the weekends. I stayed busy, not because I had to, but because I wanted to. I liked having a full calendar. I thrived at being busy and feeling productive and stretched in a lot of different ways. It wasn't just about occupying my time but pursuing goals that were important to me. Having goals gave me purpose and achieving them brought me incredible joy. You'll remember from the previous chapter that my doing things was never about having confidence, but just having the courage to go after what often felt hard. I liked doing things that felt like a challenge even though I was often shaking in my boots.

One of the first big goals I remember achieving was playing the piano for my brother's graduation. I was a freshman and he was a graduating senior. I had taken piano lessons for about 5 years and was given the opportunity to play Pomp and Circumstance as the graduating seniors, including my older brother, slowly marched in. Prior to me playing that year, I'm pretty sure the music had always been performed by much more skilled pianists; people who knew what they were doing, people who wouldn't mess up. As much as it frightened me, I decided to work towards this honorable goal. The song was quite difficult requiring me to practice like crazy. And when it came time for me to play, I was more than a little nervous.

Would I mess up?

Would I be able to recover?

Would everyone stare?

Would my brother be embarrassed?

Well, I did mess up a few times, and I did struggle a little to recover, but it didn't really matter. The graduates still marched in wearing their caps and gowns, and all eyes were on them (not me) as they proudly made their way to their seats. I was relieved when I was finally able to stop playing and focus on my brother receiving his diploma. I had done my part, and now it was his turn to shine.

After playing the piano in front of hundreds of people that night, it was there that I realized that I could not only do a lot of things, but I could do some hard things too. I could commit to something challenging, do the work to prepare for it, and finish what I set out to do. Life wasn't about just being busy, but finding inspiration, joy, and purpose along the journey of conquering fears and pursuing goals. I didn't just love achieving goals, but I loved who I became along the way.

Are you someone that always has to have something to do? Do you make countless lists, fill your calendar with plans and goals, and look forward to each new day? Do you find tremendous satisfaction in just checking things off your to-do list? Do you set goals for yourself each month or each year? Are you always working towards something big like training for a half marathon or getting a promotion? Do you love redecorating your home each season? Do you get geeked out about a new school year and buying new supplies? Are you constantly coming up with a project? Are you always learning something new? Does having a goal light your heart on fire? Are you a person that needs to feel like you are always growing and improving? Do you get just as excited about the pursuit as you do with the destination?

I am definitely one of those people I am describing above. I find myself having a bit of an achiever mindset sometimes. Goals excite me, and I feel my happiest and most fulfilled when I am in pursuit of big goals I wish to achieve. When I am not working towards something, when I feel stagnant and still, I quickly start to lose my motivation and drive. I get down on myself and others. I start feeling a bit sluggish, dissatisfied, bored, and incredibly unfulfilled.

I start slipping back into bad habits and negative coping mechanisms. I start questioning my purpose. I actually feel more anxious when I am sedentary than when I am running a hundred miles per hour towards a goal. Does that sound crazy? I am just not good at being still or simply being content with mediocracy. I am someone that always needs to be working on something that betters myself or my surroundings. I need to be in pursuit of something challenging that requires planning and work, commitment and perseverance. Having goals keeps me motivated and achieving them fills me up.

Some people think I'm out of my mind, but I actually enjoy doing really hard things like running marathons for the pure satisfaction of proving to myself that I can do it. I like challenging myself where it's me against me and no one else. If you've run a marathon, you know how incredibly difficult it is. You know the amount of training required, and you remember the all-over pain in your body as you proudly cross that finish line.

Finishing is all I ever hope to do, because running a marathon is so much more for me than a personal-record time or an award.

I don't just love the gratification that comes with completing it (or the banana or shiny medal I'm handed at the finish line), but I love the journey along the way. I get all fired up about researching races and signing up for them. I love the planning that comes along with the goal and the training (well, maybe not all the training) and dedication that is required to get my body ready. But most of all I love the person I become while pursuing the big goal. When I am working towards something, I am definitely more eager to wake up in the morning, I am more intentional about how I plan my day, and I am happier and therefore a better wife and mom to those I love. Zig Ziglar says that "what you get by achieving your goals is not as important as what you become by achieving your goals." It's all about the journey not just the finish line.

I enjoy running for exercise and my mental and emotional health, but I often need something to keep it fun and interesting. By signing up for races, whether 5K's or full marathons, it gives me something to train for. When I have a goal, I have a reason to get out there on the roads. It gives me an event to look forward to. It requires me to have a plan that I'm more likely to stick to. When I'm not signed up for anything, I tend to just get in a rut of doing the same old run 3-4 days a week. I don't push myself, and therefore I don't grow and become stronger. I start losing interest, getting slower, and not really enjoying it anymore. However, when there's a race on my calendar, I know I have to train more, run farther, and push myself harder so I can be ready for race day. I count down the weeks and days and plan my outfit, and I check the weather and all the things. My mindset shifts from needing to run to getting to run. Running is a blessing and race day is one of my favorite days.

It's the same thing with anything in life. When we are in pursuit of something important to us and have a specific goal we are working towards, we are going to put in a lot more effort than we normally would. We're going to wake up earlier, do the work, stay focused, and push harder to get to the end.

Last year I decided to write my first book. I got it in my head that I wanted to finish this dream of mine by the end of the year. Did I have the time? No. Had I ever written anything close to a book? Heck no. Did I receive any sort of education or training that prepared me to be an author? No, not really. But did I love reading books? Did I enjoy writing? Did I have it in me to figure it out as I went along? Did I really want to accomplish this big dream of mine? The answer to all of those questions was yes. So, I gave it my all. For nearly 1 year, I woke up early excited to work on my book before I left for work. I made time to pursue my goal. I wrote 1-2 hours at a time any chance I got. I researched how to write and publish a non-fiction book. I figured out how to edit and format my manuscript, create a cover (using a photo I snapped on a run with my phone), and ultimately self-publish my work.

I stayed motivated, inspired, and excited throughout the entire process. Were there some tears? Yes. But was there an enormous amount of pride as I kept growing? Absolutely. I became a more confident person along the way as I kept moving forward with courage. And when I finally held my first book in my hands, I was so incredibly proud of the end-result, but even more proud of my persistence to finish what I started. Those early mornings paid off. One word turned into 65,000 words, and my big goal came to fruition.

Lots of us have big dreams inside of us, but we fail to turn them into pursuable goals. Dreams are just ambitions that we think about, but goals are something we are actively working towards. A goal has a plan and gives us a "why" to get up and show up. It gives us momentum to keep going even when it feels hard. It fuels our motivation and drive. A goal lights our hearts on fire as we pursue it. It gives us a purpose even when the rest of our life feels uncertain. A goal doesn't necessarily have a timeline, but it definitely has a finish-line, and that finish-line is the greatest reward.

2020 is making us question our goals and our purpose. Many of us feel like we are mourning the loss of something. We've lost jobs, businesses, education, money, routines, memories, vacations, celebrations, and some have lost family members and friends to this virus. Some of us have lost hope. Some have lost a sense of identity and a "why."

We all need a sense of purpose even in the middle of this pandemic. Being in pursuit of something like a goal gives us something else to focus on, something that we CAN control, and more importantly something that gives us a "why." There are so many things that we cannot control right now, and although this year has been challenging and darn right awful for some people, it's also given us opportunities to learn and grow, pursue new passions, and tackle projects and goals we previously never had time for.

I have most certainly used this time to take on all kinds of new projects and goals. Every room and closet in our house has been cleaned, organized, or redecorated in some way (thanks to Corona and to shows like The Home Edit). We've painted and purged and simplified spaces (including our attic) that have needed some attention for a while. I've updated photo frames, and I've gotten caught up on over 3 years of digital photobooks. I'm writing this book in the middle of the pandemic, and I'm also focusing on my health. I'm setting goals for myself each month, focusing on things I CAN control instead of focusing on everything that is out of my control right now. This global pandemic, the economic crisis that it's caused, and the state of our country is out of my control, but what I can control is how I am choosing to fill my cup. And right now, I'm filling it up with goals.

What goals and ambitions do you have for yourself? What have you dreamed about for years, but haven't had the time or courage to pursue? Have you always wanted to write a book? Or start a blog? Maybe your dream is turning your hobby into an online business that you can profit from. Do you hope to some day run a marathon without dying? Do you wish you could go back to school? Change careers? Learn how to play the guitar? Open a coffee shop? (I wish!) Go on a mission trip? (Some day!) Or travel to all 50 states? (We're working on it!)

What's holding you back? What excuses do you keep giving yourself?

"I don't have time."

"I don't have enough motivation or energy or drive."

"I don't have the courage that it takes to see it through."

"I'll pursue my dream when my kids get older."

Fill up to Spill out

Now might be the perfect time to start working on turning those dreams into pursuable goals. What's important to you? What would light your heart on fire right now if you started to pursue it? What would give you such a strong "why" that you would wake up at 4:30am every morning to work on it? Is there something tugging on your heart that in pursuing it you would find true joy? Is there a passion burning inside your body that is just waiting to burst out? And would you be terribly disappointed if you got to the end of your life and still held that passion or calling inside of you, never choosing to pursue it?

Timothy Ferriss says that "someday is a disease that will take your dreams to the grave with you." Don't wait for someday. Don't wait for your kids to get older. Don't wait until you have more energy. If you have breath in your lungs, start figuring out a way to turn your dreams into your reality.

2020 and this global pandemic won't last forever. In fact, as I write this chapter, we are just a few months away from the end of the year. Another year will have come and gone, and we will wonder why we didn't use this gift of time to be acting on our ambitions. There is no better time than the present to tackle some goals. And they don't have to be big audacious goals.

Your goal doesn't have to be to run a marathon or start a new business or write your first novel, although those are really cool goals. Your goal might be to simply start walking every single day in order to live a healthier lifestyle. Think how accomplished you'll feel if you get to the end of the month and have walked for 30 minutes a day for 30 days straight. Your goal might be to clean out the pantry and refrigerator this week after months (or even years) of putting it off. Imagine how much easier meal prepping will be with an organized panty and fridge. Your goal might be to write a handwritten letter of encouragement or support to a family member or friend every week. Talk about making someone's day. My girls love getting hand-written snail mail from family and friends. It's becoming a lost art, but I think we should bring it back, right? Another goal might be to read one book a week for one month straight for the pure joy of gaining knowledge or escaping to a different era. I did that last month, and it was awesome!

Goals don't have to be big and impactful, but just personal to you. We don't pursue goals to please others, but to add happiness and purpose to our own lives. No one has to care about your goals but you.

Does it make you happy?

Does it give you purpose?

Does it bring you joy?

Does it fill your cup? Then do it!

Bob Goff says that "If we're satisfied doing what we're used to, it'll be easy to miss what we've been made for." Pursuing a goal gives us anticipation for what is possible. Goals give us hope for the future and joy in the present.

When you envision the life God made you for, what does it actually look like? Are you married with kids? Do you see yourself adopting? Do you have a job that you love? Do you learn and grow every day? Are you healthy, and do you have energy to run and play with your kids? Do you run marathons? Do you hike and explore new places? Do you have a clean and organized home? Do you volunteer at your church? Do you enjoy travel and adventure? Do you own a business? Do you write books? Are you the best stay-at-home wife and mom that you can be? Are you an awesome friend? Do you feel like you are living out God's calling and purpose for your life?

This vision for your life gives you a direction for your goals and what you should be working towards. When you really think about who you are, where you currently stand, and who you wish to become, what goals do you need to set for yourself in order to get there? What do you need to commit to in order to have the life God is calling you to live? It all starts with you and what goals are going into your cup each day.

I've done a lot of soul searching over the last several years, really trying to nail down what is most important to me. I've written down the goals that align with this person I wish to show up as, and each day I live my life in a way that is in continuous pursuit of them. First and foremost, I live my life in a way that glorifies God. If I am not focused on God and His purpose for me in this life, then nothing else really matters; not my job or the marathons or the books or the organized closets.

Fill up to Spill out

So, I am always questioning whether or not my vision aligns with my ultimate purpose. Next, I strive to be a loving, serving, and devoted wife to my husband of 18 years. Marriage is hard work, and by no means is our marriage a perfect fairytale, but we strive each day to make a great team and continue to choose each other and our family above everyone else. Just like I want to be a loving wife, I also want to be a patient and present mom for my girls. As a working mom, I've had to learn to be present where my feet are. When I'm at work, I do the best I can to care for my patients, but when I am at home, it's all about loving and serving my family. I want to be a patient, encouraging mom who has an awesome relationship with each of my girls.

My other goals are definitely less important but help to prioritize where my energy goes. I want to choose healthy over easy, investing in my health and wellness each and every day. I want to encourage others with my words as I not only care for patients in my office but create books and content for my readers. I want to establish routines and habits that serve me and my family, creating a home that is comfortable and filled with lots of love. I want to continue learning and growing every day so that I can be a better wife, mom, healthcare provider, friend, and so much more. And just for fun, my husband and I have a goal of seeing all 50 states with our girls before they permanently leave home. Traveling and seeing God's beautiful country is important to us, and we can't think of a better way to spend time with our girls.

My cup is filled with intentional goals for my life, and all of them give me a sense of purpose and direction. I know what's most important, and I have a vision and a plan that guides me. Have you taken the time to really think about God's purpose for you? Can you come up with five or ten goals that define your "why?" Are you actively pursuing them each and every day?

If someone looked at your life, would they know what you value the most? If they peeked at your calendar or your credit card statement, would it align with the life and goals you are pursuing? For example, if one of your big goals is to encourage others, would your calendar include coffee dates with friends, reminders to mail the birthday cards or letters you wrote, and would your credit card statement include gifts for loved ones, hand-lettered stickers to brighten someone else's day, or maybe donations towards a good cause? If you valued your health more than anything else, would your planner reveal all your scheduled workouts, meal plans, and therapy sessions? Would your credit card statement show things like running shoes, protein powder, a gym membership (that you actually use), and chiropractic care?

All of us need to take some time to really look at where we are spending our time, energy, and money. It's a great way to see what's actually important to us. When we're actively pursuing goals that support our calling, we are investing in a life that fills us up rather than drains us. We should fall in love with the process of chasing our goals, living each day with intention while pursuing the things that truly matter.

Realize that good things take time to grow, but our vision and goals for our life are worth the time and effort. Are we working to make a living, or are we working to build a life and make an impact? Are we staying content where we are, or are we actively pursuing the life we were made for?

Chapter 9

Fill up with wise choices

"Life is a matter of choices, and every choice you make makes you." John C. Maxwell

I grew up a farmer's daughter surrounded by tall corn fields and green tractors, grain bins and windy pastures. Farming was our way of life and being a part of that unique environment and lifestyle most definitely shaped me into the hard-working mom that I am today. Work, family, and faith were the values that were instilled in me, and I learned that the only way to have anything nice in life was to work for it. So, I started working from an early age. I didn't have to work, but instead I chose to work, wanting to have my own money to manage and save. My parents were incredibly generous and awesome and would have probably preferred that I not work so much, but it was their own work ethic that influenced mine. My parents worked hard and showed me that working hard to serve your family and the Lord was a good thing, so I wanted to work too.

In high school I decided to become a nurse, because I wanted to help people, and I grew up watching my mom work as a nurse. I was heavily influenced by her work and desire to serve others; so much that I didn't even look into other careers. I didn't visit but one small Christian university near home, and only briefly checked it out, because I knew it was the right choice for me. So many people I knew were struggling to decide on a college and a degree plan, visiting dozens of campuses and applying to half of those when I found the perfect place right down the road. I sensed that God wanted me at the University of Mary Hardin-Baylor for lots of different reasons, and I felt good about the decision that I was making (the nice scholarship helped too).

That was the first of many choices I made as I left home to pursue a life of my own. It ended up being a wise choice as attending this university led me to my husband and a lot of the friends we have today. It also led me to our church, my job, and this community we love so much. Had I not made the choice that I did over 20 years ago, I'm not sure where my life would be today.

Growing up I was lucky enough to be raised in a home where I learned about God from an early age. I grew up going to church, learning about morals and values, and my parents taught me how to work hard while honoring God. I learned right from wrong, sometimes the hard way. But the most important decision I finally made was to trust God and let Him guide me in my decisions.

Life can be complicated, but when we put our faith and trust in the Lord, the Holy Spirit lives in us and through us and helps us make the right decisions. Will we mess up? Absolutely. Will we learn from our mistakes, ask God for forgiveness and do better next time? Yes, but only if we continue to put our trust in God and God alone.

Not everyone was raised in a home like me. In fact, I would probably be right if I said that nearly half of my readers had difficult upbringings in not-so-great environments with some pretty bad experiences, and that's okay. Sometimes a challenging past is what makes us stronger. Our past does not define us. It is not a life sentence of hardship, misery, or shame. We don't have to be a product of our past, but instead make choices to build the life God created us for. What's in the past is in the past, but our future depends on each little decision we continue to make as we move forward. And the first choice we make is choosing to pursue a life that sometimes looks much different than our past.

Our upbringing as well as our environment and experiences, both good and bad, often shape us, but it's the choices we continue to make that really define us. Our past is just a small part of our story, but our future is often written by all the decisions we make. We are an active participant of our own life. Life is full of endless choices, and what a blessing it is that we get to choose a lot of what goes on those pages of our story. We have the incredible opportunity to create a life that fills us up if we make wise choices. We choose who guides us on our path as well as our actions, our attitude and effort as we journey through life. We choose our habits and routines, as well as our perspective and mindset. We choose who we surround ourselves with and how we allow them to influence our life. And we get to choose what goes into our cup and fuels us each day, so why not choose wisely?

Wise choices create positive consequences. When we choose wisely, we get closer and closer to the person God made us to be. We become a better version of ourselves each day. We start experiencing the quality of life we wish to live filled with peace, joy, and purpose.

A lot of what we do every single day are habits and routines that we've developed over time. We do them without even thinking about them. It's important that we choose wisely when building these behaviors and practices. Our choices will either fuel us or drain us. They will either give us life or destroy our life, right? The choices we make are the difference between the life we want and the life we're staying stuck in or settling for. James Clear says that "every action you take is a vote for the type of person you wish to become." We get to decide what is important, because when it's important, we figure out a way to make it part of our routines and habits.

If having good dental hygiene is important, we'll make it a habit to brush our teeth every morning and every night. If staying physically healthy is a priority, we'll take the time to prepare nutritious meals and exercise on a regular basis. If having a relationship with God is important (and it should be!), we will have a consistent routine of pursuing Him every day. If having a clean home is important, we will create habits and routines to keep it that way. If emotional and mental health is a priority, we will invest in pouring into our cup the things that bring us joy and peace instead of fear and anxiety. We choose our every action. We choose what's important and build the habits and routines around the things that we value.

Do you sometimes wonder why you don't have the life that God's called you to live? You feel stuck and frustrated, and maybe a little envious of someone else's life. They seem to have it all together when you barely keep your head above water most days. It's probably because you haven't created the right habits and routines to get you to the place you wish to be. You want to wake up early in order to not feel rushed or be late to work, but you have a habit of pushing the snooze button. You want to eat healthy meals, but instead you don't take the time to meal plan and shop, leaving you no choice but to go through the drive-thru again. You want to have a clean house like your friend does, but you frequently leave dishes in the sink at night and don't have any sort of daily and weekly cleaning routine. You want to be someone that exercises every day but watching the new Netflix series has become a part of your evening routine, leaving you no time to go for a run. So much of what we do every day is out of habit. Sometimes we don't even realize we are doing it.

Two years ago, I was able to finally break the bad habit of biting my nails. I had done it for most of my life. I wanted pretty nails, but because I was in the habit of biting them when I felt anxious or bored, I never had the nails I dreamed of. But one day, I committed to breaking the bad habit of biting them, and instead formed a new habit of taking care of them. Little by little, my nails grew out, and instead of biting them, I started giving myself a home manicure each week. In forming a new habit of filing and painting my nails, I was able to ditch the bad habit of biting them.

Fill up to Spill out

Oftentimes, you have to add a good habit in order to get rid of a bad one. Another example would be when smokers want to quit smoking and decide that they are going to take on running instead. As they start forming a new habit of running each day, they quickly realize that smoking is the thing that is holding them back, and they are able to finally ditch their unhealthy smoking habit to pursue a healthier lifestyle. By deciding to become a runner and taking the steps to do so, they are able to break the habit that is slowing them down. Runners can't be smokers just like women with pretty nails can't bite them. A lot of this stuff is just in our head, and we have to figure out how to change our mind and therefore change our habits and coping mechanisms.

As I write this chapter, I'm looking down at my unpainted nails that have once again been chewed on during several weeks of stress. I'm reminded how easy it is to slip back into bad habits when I am not focused on keeping up with the good ones. I haven't taken the time to paint my nails in the last few weeks triggering me to start chewing on them again.

We all do this. When we are not being intentional about staying on track with our good habits, we easily fall back into not-so great ones. Today, I'm going to take the time to give myself a good manicure in order to remind myself that I still want pretty nails. It's time to build a good habit and routine again in order to ditch the bad one that doesn't serve me. I need to do this with a few things in my life right now, and I bet I'm not alone.

What good habits and routines do you need to build in order to create the life you're made for? Do you wish you had more time to invest in yourself and your personal goals? Then create a habit of waking up 1-2 hours earlier in the morning. Use that time to pour into yourself and your goals while your family is still asleep. Quit pushing the snooze button and instead create a stellar morning routine that includes coffee, quiet time with the Lord, and intentional investment in the goals that are important to you.

Do you wish you could lose weight and get healthier? Then start building habits and routines around meal planning, prepping, and moving your body instead of choosing easy and convenient. Decide that you are worth the effort to get healthy and invest in the time and dedication it takes to get you there. Schedule your workouts like you schedule your child's piano lessons. Take time on Sunday to prepare your meals and snacks for the week. Instead of saying you don't have time, make the time.

Do you wish your house was clean and organized? Then work on creating new routines that will help you to get it in order and keep it that way. Take time each day to tackle one room, one closet, or one drawer. Start the dish washer each night and unload it in the morning. Fold and put away the clothes as soon as they come out of the dryer. Don't go to bed without picking up the toys and wiping down the kitchen counters. Create a consistent schedule of when you will do things like cleaning the bathrooms and changing out the sheets and stick with that schedule. It's all about systems and routines. When we stick with an effective routine, it becomes a habit, and when it's a habit, we do it without even thinking about it. Pretty soon that house will be clean, and it will stay that way because of the little actions you take every single day.

Each day we choose how we show up for ourselves and others. We choose how we start our day. We choose our mood and our attitude. We choose our perspective and our mindset. We choose to either fill our cup with positivity, joy, kindness, gratefulness, and a growth mindset or we fill it with negativity, misery, anger, and a fixed mindset. Which cup tastes like honey and naturally flows out to others in a beautiful way? And which cup tastes like a bitter beer that spills out leaving a pungent aroma? Which cup do you want? Which cup do you wish to share with others?

Our environment and experiences throughout the day have the power to affect our mood, but if we wake up choosing our mood for the day, we have a much greater chance of controlling it as things come up that try to shift it. When we choose positivity, gentleness, forgiveness, and joy each day, we look for the good in every situation. We choose to not just love the people who are kind to us, but to love the ones that are not so kind. We choose to love like Jesus. We look at a bad situation and wonder what God's teaching us through it. We look at change as opportunity. We show up with a smile, even behind these masks we're having to wear. We create our own sunshine even when there doesn't seem to be any brightness in our day. Instead of complaining, we get to work. Instead of talking, we choose to listen. Instead of spreading harsh words and reactions of anger, bitterness, and despair, we choose to spread kindness, empathy, and love.

Our mindset is also important. Do you have a fixed mindset or a growth mindset? Is your mind filled with all sorts of limiting beliefs that hold you back from being who God made you to be? Do you avoid challenges, put in fruitless effort, give up easily, and believe in fixed abilities? Or do you persevere through failures, believe that effort and determination is required to build new skills, do you embrace challenges, and desire to learn and build new abilities? Do you resist criticism and guidance, or do you welcome feedback so you can learn and improve? Do you finish what you've started, or do you stop when it gets hard? Do you focus on enjoying the journey, or do you only look for the finish line?

When we focus on growing our mind we grow in life. When we choose to stay stuck, always resisting change and challenge, our life becomes stagnant. Instead of living the life we were made for, we settle for far much less. Choosing a growth mindset is a wise choice. Choosing to learn and grow is choosing to become better. Choosing to persevere through all of life's many failures and disappointments makes us stronger. Choosing purpose over fear, effort over easy, and finishing over quitting builds character.

Who we choose to surround ourselves with is also how we grow through life. Have you ever noticed how a husband and wife actually start to look like each other over time? They finish each other's sentences and often have a lot of the same habits, good and bad. It's just like we read in scripture that the two shall become one flesh (1 Corinthians 7:1-2). We start to become more and more like the people we spend the most time with. We start to dress the same, act the same, talk the same, choose the same, and become the same. It's crucial that we surround ourselves with people who share similar values and goals for their life as we do. It's not that we can't love those who are different (and we should), but the people we spend the most time with are the ones who we start to become most like. And if we want to become our very best self, then we need to choose wisely.

I used to think that I could change people. I looked for the good in everyone, sometimes ignoring the red flags, just hoping that my positive influence might help to change them. I got burned several times. People often don't change, especially if someone is trying to make them change. Instead, we're often the ones that get pulled down when we are choosing to hang around people who don't share our same vision for life. People change when they're ready to change. We can be kind and encouraging and try to be the positive influence they need, but they are ultimately responsible for their own choices and actions. It's okay to love them as they are while not letting their personal choices influence ours. It's all about discernment.

But if you're wanting to become a better version of yourself, you need to surround yourself with people who share the same values and goals you have for your own life. Choose friends who build you up instead of tear you down. Choose the right spouse to partner with in life and never stop working on that key relationship. Choose a workplace with great culture and vibe that supports you and the things that are important to you. Choose a church that makes you feel welcome and loved while helping you grow in your faith. Choose to follow people on social media that you admire, those who model courage, kindness, and positivity. Be influenced by content that makes you want to learn and grow to become a better version of yourself.

A lot of what shows up on our social media feeds is what we have chosen to be there; people who aren't actually our real-life friends, people we used to know that no longer add value to our lives, family that never posts anything positive, media pages that only post news that is negative and fear mongering, celebrities that make us feel bad about ourselves or our bodies. Just as easy as it is to friend and follow people and their pages, it is just as easy to unfollow or mute people that make us feel unhappy, discouraged, envious, or angry. We don't have to feed our minds with content that doesn't fuel us or encourage us to be the person God made us to be. We can choose wisely by filling our cup with people and content that fuels us instead of drains us.

We choose what we put into our cup each day. We choose whether or not to fill it with darkness, folly, and discouragement

Fill up to Spill out

or to fill it with sunshine, wisdom, and encouragement. What goes in comes out, so why not fill it with an attitude of gratitude as well as a growth mindset? Our mood is a choice. Although we cannot control everything around us, what we can control is our reaction to those things. We can wake up in the morning and decide that today is going to be a good day. We can fill our cup with a grateful heart, a giving spirit, and a positive attitude. We don't have to buy into what the news is saying. We don't have to live in fear or be angry and divisive like the rest of the world. We can choose to be kind, choose to love, and choose to grow.

2020 has definitely tested our ability to continue making wise choices through difficult times. From the global pandemic and the many ways it has been handled, to politics and an important election year, to division and unrest in our country causing riots and destruction, to natural disasters and endless tragedy, this year has been challenging. There has been so much change, so much hardship for working families, varying degrees of sadness and loss, and incredibly difficult decisions each day. But through all of the disappointment, fear, and uncertainty we still get to choose how we react, respond, and continue to serve. We get to choose how we learn from all of this. We get to choose how we use our time, where we put our energy, and who we love on with our God-given purpose and gifts. We choose how we process this season, how we remember it, and how we grow from it all.

We still have choices. We get to choose what is best for our family. We choose how we show up at work. We choose how we continue to grow our faith when churches are closed or meeting differently. We choose how we stay connected with family and friends when social distancing limits how we gather. We choose how we support our small businesses when they are not allowed to operate in their usual way. We choose how we educate our children in the middle of a global pandemic. We choose how we encourage our teachers and school administrators as they navigate an incredibly different and demanding kind of school year. We choose how we return to a sense of normalcy after going through a very abnormal time.

Joe Tichio says that "every choice you make is creating your future. Choose wisely." What kind of future do you envision for yourself? Who did God create you to be, and do you have some work to do in order to be that best version of yourself? All we get in life is time and choices, and some of those choices can literally change the trajectory of our entire life if we choose wisely. So, I encouraged you to keep filling your cup with wise choices.

Chapter 10

Fill up by encouraging others with your gifts

"The meaning of life is to find your gift. The purpose of life is to give it away."

Pablo Picasso

One of the best things I've done over the last 8 years is serve as a preceptor and mentor for nurse practitioner students in my clinic. As they are going through their master's program and training to do what I do, they basically knock on doors and send cold-call emails to anyone who will possibly agree to precept them during their clinical hours. That's right. They have to find their own preceptors, and it's certainly no easy task. I remember it all too well as a NP student myself, searching for someone to mentor and train me. I ended up having to drive 45 minutes each way to a clinic where I found someone that would take me. He was tough, and I definitely shed some tears on the way home most days, but I learned and grew, and I am eternally grateful for his time, wisdom, and mentorship along my journey to do what I do today.

Serving as a preceptor is definitely a tough job with absolutely no compensation and very little acknowledgment, but it's a great way to give back to a profession that you care about. I've said yes to at least 10 students over the years, committing to teach and mentor them for thousands of hours during my busy workday. I've basically done it out of the kindness of my heart, teaching them everything I know (and don't know) and encouraging them on their educational journey to becoming a healthcare provider. Each student has been very different, a few pretty exhausting for me, but overall it has been such a rewarding part of my practice. It feels good to be needed. It's fun to share what I know and encourage others with my knowledge and experience.

I remember what it was like to be a student. Some days were absolutely brutal. I left clinicals in a bucket of tears feeling dumb and discouraged, not sure if I wanted to return the following day. A teacher and mentor can make you or break you, and mine definitely tried to break me (or so I thought). Thankfully, I came out stronger and smarter.

As a somewhat seasoned nurse practitioner now, I never want my students to feel that way. School is hard enough, and they don't need one more person making them feel inadequate, but instead someone that lifts them up and encourages them. I don't just mentor them but become friends and colleagues with them along the way. I'm always a little sad when our time comes to an end. Serving as a preceptor and encouraging others with my gifts is such a rewarding part of my job, and I'm glad I get to do it.

In the last few chapters, I've talked about the importance of having goals and creating purpose in our lives, but an even bigger part of living the life we're made for is encouraging those around us. We have unique abilities and talents that are just waiting to be shared. Our words and our actions have incredible influence for someone, and we need to find ways to use them to make a positive impact, whether it's at home, at work, or next door. We should make it our mission to encourage and lift up others each and every day.

The key to really feeling satisfied in life is understanding why we are here and who we are serving and encouraging with our purpose. If we don't know the answer to that, then we aren't truly living the life we were made for but going through the motions of life and simply just existing. We were created for so much more than just a life of existence. God made us to do more than just eat and breathe and merely survive. We are here to thrive. Each season, we should know what our purpose is and who we are serving with that purpose. And you know what? It's going to keep changing. As God's people, we are constantly growing and evolving. As seasons change, so do we. Our purpose and who we are serving with it keeps changing too, and that's a good thing. Afterall, none of us wants to be stuck in the stage of raising toddlers our entire life, right?

Our purpose might go from growing our education while being a good friend and serving as a camp counselor, to growing our career and family with a focus on being the best mom to our kids. As our kids leave home, our purpose might include adding some volunteer work and serving more at church. We might focus on being a loving grandparent or a caregiver for our aging parent or spouse. During a difficult season like we are going through right now, we might decide to write a book that encourages others. We might want to start a new business or a non-profit that serves the community. We might choose to show up on social medial encouraging others through blogging and photography just to be a light in a season of darkness. Just know that as seasons change, so do we. Our gifts and talents change. Our purpose changes. Our focus changes. The people we love and serve changes too.

Every job I've had in life so far has involved working with people. I've worked behind a cash register, pushed grocery carts, waited on diners at a restaurant, worked weddings, been a nurse on a busy hospital floor, and I've currently been in my role as a nurse practitioner for over 12 years. I interact with people every single day. Working with people is not always easy (did you know that not all people are kind?), but it's what I do. Each day I get up and go to a job that allows me to care for others. Every job I've had over the last 25 years (wow, that makes me sound old) has been about serving others in one way or another. It's a big part of who I am and why I'm here, but it's not my only calling or purpose. I'm a follower of Christ, a wife, a mom, a writer, and more. Within each of these roles, I have purpose and people to serve with my purpose. I'm constantly looking for new ways to encourage others with my growing gifts and talents.

We can all be trained and educated to do a particular job that provides for our family and serves others in some way, but our jobs are not our only purpose. Yes, a lot of us spend an enormous amount of time doing our jobs and serving the people that are affected by our work, but our occupation is not our only calling. We work to pay the bills, and yes it gives us something to do and someone to serve, but there are plenty of other ways to love and encourage others too.

Being a loving spouse, an intentionally present mom, a good homemaker, a helpful daughter, an encouraging friend, a reliable accountability partner, or a dependable volunteer are all examples of where we can also find purpose. Some of you might not have a job outside the home like me, but you are the most loving, supportive wife, hands-on mom, and organizer of all the things. That is your purpose, and you fully embrace it, and I think that's awesome. Some of you might be retired but are volunteering a lot of your time at the free clinic and doing an awesome job at being the best nana for your grandkids. Your purpose depends on what season of life you are in and what your focus is on. Just because you don't have a J-O-B you go to every day does not mean that you don't have purpose. We all have purpose.

Sometimes it's not our careers or our typical roles that give us purpose, but a special calling or identity that we choose to pursue on our own time. Maybe it's something unexpected and outside the box. Maybe it's writing books when the rest of the house is asleep. Maybe it's starting an online business that uses your beautiful handwriting to create words of affirmation on stickers and window clings that remind your community who they were made to be. Maybe it's selling shirts to provide food for hungry kids. Maybe it's going on mission trips to serve people abroad.

We are all born with these unique gifts and talents, ideas and passions, and have dreams inside of us just waiting to be pursued. We have things that we are good at. We have ideas about how to make things better. We have a book inside of us waiting to get on paper. We have creativity that needs to come out. We have a voice that needs to be heard. We have a light that needs to shine.

But fear is what sometimes holds us back from pursuing this type of calling. Fear stops us from sharing some of our gifts with others. We let fear override our purpose. We let the opinions of others hold us back. We doubt ourselves and our big dreams. We compare our little accomplishments to others with more success. We stop when it feels hard. Or we never get started in the first place. Instead we settle for convenient and expected, easy and small, instead of having the courage to go after the ambitious thing that what would result in overwhelming growth and fulfillment.

What's burning a hole inside of you right now? What is it, and who would it serve? What calling has God put on your heart that in pursuing it would give you a new purpose and impact a community of people who need it? Do you feel like your life is missing a purpose? Do you hunger and thirst for more? Are you wanting to make more of an impact? Are you not fulfilled in your current job or role at home? Is the season you're walking in making you feel like you don't have a purpose or anyone to share it with?

Let me just say that everyone has a purpose, and there is always someone that needs to be encouraged with our gifts. Just because someone else has already done it, wrote it, or spoke it doesn't mean that you can't do it too. Your way of doing it, writing it, or speaking is unique to you and will encourage a new and different group of people. Fear shouldn't stop you from having the courage to pursue the calling of your heart. Self-doubt or the opinions of others doesn't have to keep you in a box. Instead, you need to go after your dreams, find purpose in something different, and encourage others in a new and exciting way.

Having purpose gives us something to fill our day with but encouraging others with that purpose is what truly gives us life.

We feel most fulfilled when what we are doing is having a positive impact on others; when we can see that what we are doing matters, and when we live a life that is not just about living and breathing but helping others. This can be done in lots of different ways.

Covid-19 has resulted in a lot of people feeling like they have lost their sense of identity and purpose, especially if that purpose was wrapped up in the entertainment industry, restaurant business, church, sports, travel, or teaching kids inside of a classroom setting. So many people's jobs have been affected by the change and uncertainty inside this new world we are living in.

As a healthcare provider, I have had patients tell me that they feel stuck at home and don't know what their purpose is in this crazy season. Teachers feel discouraged as they can't be in the classrooms with their students. The travel and entertainment industries are not only suffering tremendous financial loss, but the people who work inside those industries have lost their sense of purpose. Churches have had to go virtual, making ministering to others more difficult. Everyone has had to pivot and get creative in how they are not only making a living, but how to have purpose and serve others in a new and challenging time. Some businesses and jobs haven't been able to survive while others have figured out a new way to thrive.

In my clinic, I get to visit with people all day long. I hear from patients who are really struggling through this season, who have barely left their house in over 6 months, who haven't physically seen a single family member for fear of catching the virus, and people who have lost their purpose since they are no longer able to work or volunteer due to the current situation. It saddens me to think that they feel all alone, that they have let fear become so much stronger than their purpose. They have chosen to just sit at home and be lonely instead of figuring out ways to use this time to do something else that might encourage others. Instead of looking for the silver linings in all of this, they do nothing but wait and complain and feel lost.

And just like I hear from this group of people who feel alone and purposeless and can't figure out how to thrive, I also see the opposite from a different group of patients. When this pandemic first started, there were groups and individuals who got busy sewing masks, delivering hundreds and hundreds of masks to local clinics and hospitals, nursing homes and other places that so desperately needed them. Our clinic was on the receiving end of this kindness from a lot of our patients. We received masks and hand sanitizer and other items that the community felt we needed. What a blessing it was to see such thoughtful encouraging people using their extra time to serve others.

People have continued to find all sorts of creative ways to love and serve during this trying time, from shopping for neighbors and loved ones, to putting "healthcare hero" signs in people's yards, to writing encouraging words on their social media, and painting up the windows all over town. Our sweet neighbor gave us a dozen eggs when they were extremely hard to find. Others offered toilet paper and cleaning wipes. It's crazy how much you appreciate something when you can no longer find it. Who would have ever thought we would be searching all over town for toilet paper in the middle of a pandemic?

Other patients of mine have been using this time to be productive, cleaning, organizing, and decluttering their house, donating unwanted clothing to groups who need it. They've been doing home projects and planting gardens and working on their health goals. I've had patients actually lose weight and improve their diabetic numbers, because now they've had time to focus on their diet and exercise. Others have told me about writing letters to pen-pals in nursing homes, sending care packages to their grandchildren, and organizing boxes of old photos. I enjoy hearing about all the many ways people have used their time, how they've created purpose for themselves, and how they've loved and served in various ways.

This time is a beautiful opportunity if you choose to see it that way. People need encouragement more than ever. People need to feel seen and heard, to be valued and appreciated, and to be inspired. Essential workers have been going to work this entire time. A thank you goes a long way. Teachers are having to learn a new way to teach and are returning to work with masks and social distancing to try and keep everyone safe. They need to feel supported. Leaders are making really tough decisions. They need our prayers and buckets full of endless grace. Students are feeling lost and disappointed. They need to be loved on and encouraged through this very strange time. So many people are being affected by this pandemic, and there are so many ways to serve them.

You may have lost your job or your favorite hobby or your ability to travel or maybe you lost your moment on stage when you were supposed to graduate with honors, but there are plenty of amazing opportunities to still have purpose and make beautiful memories with your family and friends. This time is all about getting creative, about pivoting and changing, and taking this sour lemon we were given and turning it into thirst quenching lemonade. Our local art studio that I adore has had to pivot several times during this season. They normally offer in-studio classes, painting, parties, and events, but due to Covid they had to start offering virtual classes and art to-go. The owner of the studio was the one that went all over town, painting windows of businesses with beautiful hearts and the words, "we are all in this together." What a thoughtful way to spread joy during a time of uncertainty.

It doesn't take much to encourage someone who needs it. A hand-written note, a sweet text message early in the morning, some home-made cookies, a phone call, a care package with goodies, a gift card for coffee, donuts for the office, or a hug to show you care (yes, we still need to hug even during a pandemic). Your purpose in this season might simply be to encourage others.

As a healthcare worker who has been going to work this entire time, wearing a mask all day, learning new ways of doing things and interacting with people who are not always the kindest, encouragement goes a long way. Hearing patients say thank you for working right now, thank you for putting your health and your family's health on the line for us, thank you for being available, thank you for checking on me, and thank you for everything you are doing here to keep us safe makes my job so rewarding. Other workers need encouragement too. Our grocery workers, our Amazon delivery drivers, our postal workers, our educators, our pastors, and our small business owners need our support. We all need more kindness, grace, and encouragement during a year filled with challenge.

Fill up to Spill out

Each of us are blessed with gifts just waiting to impact others. Filling our cup looks like using our unique purpose to serve and encourage others. Don't you feel so much better when you do good for others? Doesn't it make you smile to be the bright spot in someone else's day? Isn't it better to give than to receive? Having purpose is important but having someone to serve with that purpose gives us an abundant life.

Allison R. Smith

Chapter 11

Fill up with Jesus

"Fill your bucket with love and you become love." Bob Goff

When I was growing up, like most people young in their faith, I questioned mine from time to time. It was hard for me to understand the importance of a relationship that I didn't truly feel. Afterall, how do we put all of our trust in a God that we cannot see? How do we know He really exists? How do we know that the Bible and the stories in it are real? How can we be sure that God is hearing and answering our prayers? Why would God allow bad things to happen to the people He loves? Like *really* bad things to *really* good people? Some things just didn't make sense to me, and I bet it's safe to say that you too have questioned your faith and the realness of your Creator and Savior in different seasons of your life. Afterall, we're human, and it's natural to question things we don't fully understand.

My grandma was often the one who would remind me of why we know God is real. She would marvel over a new baby, looking at his fingers and toes, appreciating the miracle of life that grew inside a woman's body. When she met and held each of my baby girls, she pointed out every little feature, amazed at how God created eyes to see, ears to hear, and hands to touch. She would often grab my hand when we were together, thanking God for all my hands could do. She was brought to tears just admiring the intricacies of the human hand, saying that only God could design us with such care and attention to details.

She and my grandpa traveled all around the country seeing each of the 50 states and quite a few countries too, bringing home beautiful pictures to share with the family. When she spoke of how amazing it was to see the world, she would thank God for creating such beauty and magnificence. She thanked Him for the rain and for sunshine, for rainbows and stars. She reminded me that only God could think up such incredible details for us to enjoy. "If we don't believe in the God of creation, then who put the stars in the sky?" she would ask.

I miss my grandma so much. I miss her beautiful icy blue eyes that shed tears whether she was happy or sad. I miss her smile and her laughter, her welcoming voice and warm hugs as we walked through the squeaky back door that led us to her kitchen. I miss her cooking and hospitality, her fried okra and homemade pies. I miss her hand-written letters and greeting cards for every holiday. I miss her storytelling at Christmas time and her phone calls that often abruptly ended when she decided it was time to say goodbye. I miss her presence at every major event in my life. I miss her being a great-grandmother to my girls. But most of all I miss her little reminders that God is very real, that our faith is what is most important in life, and that we should thank God for everything. "Thank you, thank you, thank you God," she would often say each time we were together.

Several years before the only grandma I knew passed away, my mom purchased a recordable book for each of the great grandkids at the time. She had my grandma read each book, recording her unforgettable voice on every page. The book was titled, "Thank God for everything." How appropriate for someone that truly thanked God for everything in her life. The book was special then as she gifted it to each child, but what a treasure it is now to hear her familiar voice after she is no longer with us. What an impact she had on all of our lives and still does today as I write this, remembering all the ways she blessed me.

Our faith is important as we journey through this thing called life. No matter what seasons we walk through, beautiful or hard, it is our faith that truly keeps us grounded, centered, and focused. God is the one who loves us, guides us with His light, comforts us through scripture, and strengthens us during our days on Earth. When we grow our faith in God, we grow our love for others; not just our love for our family and friends, but our love for *all* people. When our faith is strong, our impact is stronger. We aren't just focused on a life that is pleasing to us, but a life that is pleasing to God. It's important that we fill our cup with Jesus. God sent his son Jesus to teach us how to love others. He loved *all* people, so much that He died on the cross for our sins. When we fill our cup with that kind of sacrificial love, it can't help but spill out to others.

Growing our faith starts with surrendering our lives to Him. When we have lovingly committed our lives to following Jesus, we understand the importance of a lifelong relationship with Him. This journey includes spending time getting to know Him, worshiping Him, and allowing Him to slowly transform our minds and our hearts. A transformed heart filled with Jesus results in a transformed life. Romans 12:2 (NIV) says "Do not conform any longer to the pattern of this world but be transformed by the renewing of your mind."

I remember growing up thinking that baptism and good works somehow got me to Heaven. I'm not sure if it was what I was taught in church or simply how I interpreted it (probably the latter), but my thinking was oh so wrong. Spending eternity with Christ has nothing to do with being baptized as a child or doing good works for the Lord, but simply choosing to follow Jesus. It's a choice to place your trust in Him and Him alone, to grow your faith and have that personal relationship with your Creator and Savior. It's asking the Lord for guidance in your life. It's choosing to be more like Him. Good works alone do not get us to Heaven, but rather what's in our heart, and that's Jesus.

Attending church is an excellent place to start growing your faith and building a long-lasting relationship with Jesus. It's not a requirement to be a follower of Christ, but it's a great way to be part of a faith community. In church you find a group of believers to worship with as well as opportunities to learn and grow, love and serve with others. It's definitely something that fills my cup each week.

But if you didn't grow up in church or have left the church for various reasons, finding a church that feels right can take time. Every church is incredibly different, and just because you didn't feel welcome or connected at one church, doesn't mean you won't find a church that fits your needs. I would encourage you to try out different churches in your community, get plugged in, and find a church you look forward to attending week after week. It's not about choosing a certain denomination or pastor but finding a place that focuses on Jesus. Be poured into, but also be generous with your time, talents, and money to serve the church, the community and areas abroad. When you spend time at church each Sunday, it truly prepares your heart for the rest of the week.

Church is a good thing, but it's not the only thing. Our cup doesn't stay full if we are not also spending time with Jesus during the rest of our week. We need more than just Sunday mornings. Growing our faith also looks like making time for Bible study, scripture writing, morning devotional, prayer, and service to others. It looks like the music we listen to in our homes and in our cars, the conversations we have with others, the things we invest our time in, and the people we choose to love on.

Growing our faith in God doesn't require a huge amount of time each day, just consistency. Two years ago, I developed a morning routine that changed my life and my walk with Christ. Starting my day with a daily devotional, a gratitude practice and time to set my intentions for the day has been the key to improving the way I live my life. I am happier, more content, more fulfilled, and just more excited about being the person God made me to be.

Fill up to Spill out

Our quiet time with the Lord is important. It helps us start our day on the right foot, focus our thoughts and intentions, and align our actions with God's desire for us.

But this morning routine didn't come easy at first. 4:30am is early. It's easy to talk yourself out of it. However, if you have an important enough reason to wake up early, you will do it. If you find value in what you're doing, you'll keep doing it. You'll actually start anticipating your alarm and wake up before it even goes off in the morning. It's kind of like when you have to get up for an early morning flight for vacation or even on Christmas morning. You jump right out of bed the moment the alarm goes off, right? Or better yet, your eyes pop open before the alarm even sounds. For my husband, it's hunting season. Nothing gets him out of bed on a cold, dark Saturday morning like the anticipation of going deer hunting at the lease.

Growing your faith matters, and it all starts with you. Try spending some time with Jesus before the rest of your day gets started. Make that time so sacred that you don't mind getting up when it's still dark outside. Do it for a week and watch your faith journey grow. Fill your cup with Jesus so you can spill out His love to others.

Allow me to paint a picture of a week of filling your cup with Jesus. Imagine going to church on a Sunday morning, serving in the nursery for an hour or greeting people as they come through the doors. Then you and your family or friends go to worship, sing songs that light your heart on fire, pray for your community and your country, study scripture together that feels perfectly timed for what is going on in your life. Then you leave church and go enjoy some delicious lunch with friends who give you the fuel you need to take on the rest of the week. Imagine starting each morning with about 5 or 10 minutes of prayer, Bible reading, or enjoying a quick devotional with a cup of coffee before the chaos of the day begins. Jot down 5 or 10 things that you are grateful for, while setting your goals and intentions for the day.

Is your goal to encourage those around you?

Is your goal to be a loving, patient, present wife and mom?

Is your goal to eat dinner around the table as a family each night?

Is your goal to read an encouraging book this week?

To move your body everyday?

To enjoy a much-needed date night to connect with your spouse?

To go on more family walks around the neighborhood?

Now imagine listening to Christian music or a motivational podcast on your way to work each morning, grounding your day in positivity. Picture yourself loving and serving others with your purpose as you pull from your bucket filled with Jesus. Imagine taking a walk on your lunch break, being grateful for God's beautiful creation as the warm sun hits your face and brings you peace. Visualize yourself coming home in the evening and eating dinner with your family and thanking God for the food on the table before digging in. And lastly, picture yourself going to bed at night, praying with your children as you kiss them goodnight. Doesn't that sound like living out your faith? Does the picture I painted for you sound like the life you are currently living or the life you desire?

I wish our days and weeks always looked like this, but just like you and your family, we too are a work in progress. Our prayer life could definitely be stronger. What I do know is that small steps lead to big changes. These simple actions can change your day, your week, and your entire perspective on life. Colossians 2:7 says "Let your roots grow down into Him, and let your lives be built on Him. Then your faith will grow strong in the truth you were taught, and you will overflow with thankfulness."

The Lord works in our hearts and minds to grow us to be more like Him. When we are growing our faith, we become more and more like Him. We love better, serve better, and do better. Bob Goff says that "our problem following Jesus is we're trying to be a better version of us, rather than a more accurate reflection of Him." I am definitely guilty of this, as I started this book with sharing about my desire to become the best version of myself and to live my best life. What I've learned is that our focus shouldn't be on ourselves, but on Him and who He made us to be. Our very best version of ourself looks like Jesus. And living our best life looks like a life filled with peace, joy, and purpose.

Fill up to Spill out

What we fill our cup with is what spills out to others. Filling up with Jesus looks like filling our cup with hope, love, courage, kindness, patience, empathy, forgiveness, and grace, and spilling that goodness out to the world.

2020 has really tested our faith and hope in Jesus. It's a year that just doesn't seem to want to stop. A global pandemic, wearing a mask for 6 months (or more) with no end in sight, division and unrest in a movement for racial justice, political nonsense, economic crisis, divorces happening faster than I can count, friends getting sick with this virus, hurricanes and forest fires destroying lives, and then the sudden loss of a child as I'm writing this chapter after only finding out she had cancer 2 weeks prior; a beautiful daughter of a friend, a child who loved the Lord with all her heart. Why God, why? Why are you allowing all these bad things to happen? Why are you not answering our prayers? Are you even there, God?

I'm reminded that having faith is trusting God in all of life's storms, trusting Him not just in lightness but in darkness too. It's not our job to ask why but to just trust that there's a purpose in everything that happens, and God will reveal it to us if we choose to look for it. In time God heals, reveals, rebuilds and restores. We often don't understand why these terrible things happen. We just have to walk by faith during the unexpected twists and turns of life even when we cannot see what His purpose is. In time the pain won't feel so heavy and some lightness will be restored. As Proverbs 3:5 says, "Trust in the Lord with all your heart, and do not lean on your own understanding."

As churches have been forced to shut their doors during this pandemic, as they've been deemed non-essential and high-risk for Covid-19 spread, we've been reminded that our faith has never been dependent on the church building or the pastors or teachers in it. But rather, we are the church. We are God's people. Our relationship with Christ and our hope and trust in Him is what matters.

Covid-19 has definitely disrupted a lot of our rhythms and routines, including our Sunday church time. I miss volunteering in the nursery with my girls, shaking hands with the sweet old man greeting people at the front door, worshipping our Savior with our church community, and eating brunch with family and friends afterwards. Online church is just not the same. Meeting in the parking lot wearing masks is just not the same. Having church at a football stadium with social distancing is not the same. But Jesus is still the same. As it says in Hebrews 13:8, "Jesus Christ is the same yesterday and today and forever." We've always needed Christ in our lives, but I think 2020 is showing us just how desperately we need Him. God uses certain situations to open up our eyes, and I think He is using this year to do so.

As opinions are loud and everyone seems to have a big one these days, our love is what needs to speak louder. We have a choice on how we react and respond to everything that is going on this year. We decide what we post on social media and how we choose to respond to things that disappoint us or that we don't agree with. We can add to the endless negativity and anger, fear mongering and cyberbullying, or we can be the change we wish to see. We can post, comment, and share encouragement and positivity. We can choose to love like Jesus. And sometimes loving people is simply biting our tongue or in the case of social media, pausing our typing.

Several months ago, in the midst of this already upside-down year, one of my favorite online community couples announced their shocking decision to end their marriage. Like many loyal followers and fans, I found myself commenting how shocked and disappointed I was by their statement. I truly was dumbfounded and couldn't understand how a couple that appeared to have it all together could be choosing this for their family and their business. It made me sad for not only their kids, but for the community they had worked so hard to build. In a way, it made me question everything they had previously stood for. If they couldn't make it, then how could anything they produce help others? Was it all fake and for financial gain? Had I been duped?

Later that day, as I read through some of the other comments, which were mostly negative and nasty, a few comments stood out. Instead of bashing the couple for their decision or asking why, they simply commented that they loved them so much and they were sending buckets of love and prayers during a difficult time. It was a lesson for me that day. God was reminding me that just

Fill up to Spill out

like me, these people were also human. I could have initially shown up with love for a couple who had provided me and millions of followers with inspiring content and motivational tools for years, but like a lot of people, I chose to show up with questions and comments, judgement and shame. I quickly went back and deleted my previous comment, vowing to only react with love in the future. As a follower of Jesus, I wanted to be different.

I wouldn't have to wait long, as the following month, two more of my favorite online couples also announced their plans for divorce during a year that kept on taking. Again, I was shocked and disappointed by the sad news, but this time I responded much differently. I simply wrote that I was sending love and prayers. I extended grace instead of my opinion. I loved like Jesus.

As my faith has grown stronger over the years, God has continued to help me to hold my opinion and instead choose love. I've learned this in real life (often the hard way) as well as online. It's not our job to judge or mock someone for their personal decisions whether it's our family, real-life friends, or people we think we know on the internet. It shouldn't be our mission to make our opinions louder, but instead our love and empathy greater. If we wouldn't respond this way in person (and we shouldn't), then it's not okay to do this online. Just because we can type it doesn't mean we should. It's like the old saying goes, "If you don't have anything nice to say, don't say anything at all."

Life is hard enough without the loud and rude opinions of others. Decisions are sometimes impossible and doing so in the spotlight definitely makes it harder. Whether someone says something to our face or shares it on a social media platform, we should respond like Jesus would. We should respond with grace, kindness, and love. When we fill our bucket with Jesus, we spill out with love for others. What an important lesson I learned in this tough season. One of the many, many lessons.

Allison R. Smith

Conclusion

As this book is coming to an end, I hope that you don't feel like you have to do it all and be it all in order to be the best version of yourself or live your very best life. I hope that you don't feel overwhelmed or not good enough just as you are today. You're doing a good job, and I see you and hear you and empathetically feel the busy season that you are walking through. I am walking through it too, and some days are hard.

So, if you are currently in a season where you barely feel like you are keeping your head above water, don't feel like you suddenly need to start waking up 2 hours earlier to write a book, train for a marathon, organize your closets, or start reading 4 books a month. The idea of filling up to spill out is not about adding more to your already busy-filled life, but rather evaluating what is working for you and what's not. It's about focusing on what truly matters. It's about saying no to the things that don't bring peace, joy, and purpose to your life, and instead filling up with the things that do.

Filling your cup doesn't mean you have to fill it with all the things that I've talked about in the chapters of this book. These are the actions that have helped me to live my best life, but you may thrive in a completely different way. What's most important is that you know what fills you up, and you do it every single day. I am simply encouraging you to pour some of what your pour into others back into yourself. Don't deplete yourself by only serving the needs of others, but spend some time investing in the stuff that refuels and restores you. Take time to fill your cup each day. Invest in self-care in order to love the person God made you to be. Create order and simplicity in your home and in your life to make things easier. Find community to do life with. Make time for both fun and rest. Grow yourself in order to grow others. Choose courage in order to gain confidence. Pursue goals that are important to you. Build habits and routines that serve you and those you love. Protect your peace, find joy in the little things, and discover purpose in every season. Understand why you are here and who you are serving with your gifts. And most importantly, grow your faith in God so you can love more like Jesus.

Don't feel guilty about taking time to refuel. Don't apologize for investing in yourself. Instead, have courage to grow into the person God made you to be. Show your kids that not only does their health matter, but your health matters too. Be a positive example to those who are watching. Let them see you working on your passions and goals, waking up early to read your Bible, investing in your marriage, going for runs after dinner, and enjoying an occasional girl's night with your friends. In seeing you invest in things that are important to you, they too will grow up knowing how to fill their cup.

I know you have heard it a dozen times now, but we can't pour from an empty cup. We can't live a life of purpose and impact if we never take time to pour into ourselves. John Maxwell says, "growing yourself enables you to grow others." We must grow in order to serve. Are you going to bloom into a beautiful strong woman who is a blessing to others? Or are you going to let busyness, fear, guilt, and excuses keep you from growing into the person God made you to be? The choice is yours. And I hope that you'll choose to fill up to spill out, taking little steps to be the best version of yourself that shows up well for those who need you.

Fill up to Spill out

I didn't plan on writing this book in the middle of a global pandemic, but now that I'm wrapping it up, I can definitely see why God pushed me to keep writing it. It's been a hard year, and writing has helped me process it all in real time. As I wrote each chapter during this crazy year, God was teaching me all about perspective, growing my faith, and cultivating peace, joy and purpose through my own challenges and disappointments.

I was terribly disappointed that I didn't get to see my husband walk across that stage to be formally hooded and celebrated as a Doctor of Education. I had pictured it in my mind for 6 long years, maybe even more than he did. I imagined tears streaming down my face as his name was called and the family cheered. I envisioned the pictures we'd take on Baylor's campus, the dinner we'd eat, and the big party we'd have with family and friends. Instead, a box showed up on our doorstep with his diploma, 2020 tassel, and the program that we would have received had his graduation ceremony actually happened. 6 years of hard work and sacrifice wrapped up in a simple box delivered to our front door by a postal worker. It made me sad, and I'm sure he was sad too, even though he never said so.

I was disappointed that my 5th grader's last year of elementary school ended so abruptly with no final field trips, parties, awards ceremonies, or field day. Instead our girls were forced to sit at home for 6 long months with no school, sports, and little contact with friends. I was disappointed that we didn't get to go to 3 weddings we looked forward to attending. I was sad we didn't get to go on the trips we had planned on taking, including the one to Germany. I was disappointed that I didn't get to run in several races that I was looking forward to running in and that our alma mater's fall football season was cancelled. I was sad about all the things I was forced to cross off my calendar, and I wasn't alone in feeling the disappointment. Everyone experienced varying levels of sadness and loss in 2020, whether it was the loss of expectations, events like senior prom or graduation, much anticipated trips, wedding celebrations, jobs, businesses, or even loss of family members and friends.

But something I gained in all of this was perspective. As I processed my own feelings of loss, I saw others losing so much more. I saw people losing family members to the virus, losing their homes to one natural disaster after another, losing their businesses due to riots and protests and economic crisis, and then a friend losing her daughter to cancer only weeks after getting the heartbreaking diagnosis. In the midst of an already difficult year, losing a child was the absolute worst thing I could possibly imagine. It broke my heart into a million pieces. And this wasn't the only family I knew who lost a child in 2020. Weeks later, a co-worker of mine lost his son in a tragic car accident. Why God, why?

As I watched others go through incredible loss this year, God was teaching me all about perspective, and it's something I'll never forget. It's not that their greater loss diminished my own feelings of loss but rather put things into perspective for me. Yes, we missed out on celebrations, anticipated plans, and expectations, but we could've lost so much more.

2020 was a really tough year for a lot of people. It was a year filled with forced change, tremendous disappointment, and buckets of uncertainty as we blindly navigated through uncharted territory. There was chaos and heartbreak, sickness and death. There were lost jobs and businesses, and challenges in educating our children. We experienced loss of church and community, and a disturbance of our rhythms and routines. There was cancelling and postponing of large events including weddings and graduations. There were travel restrictions and quarantines, masks and social distancing. We witnessed empty shelves and a shortage of toilet paper of all things. There was loss of identity and purpose, break-ups and divorce, cancer diagnoses and unexpected deaths. It was a year filled with racial injustices and division of our country, protests and riots, and strong opinions. There were fires and hurricanes, and political agendas in the midst of an election year like no other. As I've seen on a lot of t-shirts, "2020 was very bad, would not recommend," and I'm sure you'd agree.

But as terrible as the year was, 2020 was also good if you were looking for the silver linings. 2020 brought families together like never before as there was suddenly more time at home with quiet evenings for neighborhood walks and chats. People found simple joys in baking bread and cookies and putting puzzles together as

Fill up to Spill out

most forms of entertainment were cancelled. Bike riding, outdoor recreation, home improvement projects and creative outlets provided a much-needed distraction in the midst of the chaos. New puppies and babies were brought into homes, giving everyone something to love on. Businesses found themselves pivoting into new directions, bringing goods and services to people in a suddenly contact-free world. Goals were reevaluated, and people started focusing on the things that truly mattered.

Good change happened that needed to happen. We learned how to walk through 2020 with purpose over fear, to face each day with courage and grace, kindness and resilience, and to focus on the things that we *could* control like filling our cup so we could spill out to others.

When I look back on 2020, I will definitely remember Covid-19 and the health and economic crisis it caused, the masks and social distancing, all the change and division, disappointment and loss, but I will also remember the good. I published my first book and wrote another one that will be a great reminder of this difficult year. I ran my 3rd marathon for my 40th birthday with my husband and girls cheering me on, and then we rushed home to shower and take family pictures on our favorite college campus. We celebrated my husband's huge accomplishment of finishing his doctorate degree with a fish fry, cake, and fireworks at my older brother's house. We saw the Grand Canyon with our girls, went on our 11th annual beach trip with friends despite the fear of Covid, and we took pictures in front of Mount Rushmore during an election year like no other.

We will remember decorating Ted's new office at a brand-new middle school as he tirelessly prepared for return to school in the middle of the pandemic. We will remember church at the football stadium, Covid-style birthday celebrations with card my yard and drive-by parades, chalked-up driveways with colorful encouraging messages, purple and turquoise hair tips since it was the longest spring break ever, chats with our neighbors as our dogs played together, summer camp that looked much different but was still just as impactful, and we'll remember fishing at the creek and making special memories with our kids during quarantine.

Allison R. Smith

2020 was such a teachable year. Would we simply survive or find a way to thrive through the change? Would we cower or rise up? Would we choose anger or love? Fear or courage? Negativity or positivity? Would we fail or would we grow? Would we turn away from the church as buildings were forced to close their doors, or would we *be* the church? Would we fill our cup, or would we let our cups run dry when life went crazy? Would we spend the year wishing everything was different, or would we find a way to cultivate peace, joy, and purpose in the midst of our disappointment and frustration?

One particular song, Evidence by Josh Baldwin, really spoke to me in 2020. Even through a tough year and a challenging season, this song reminded me that there is still so much goodness all over my life, because God's promises still remain the same. Allow me to share a few of the lyrics with you.

All throughout my history

Your faithfulness has walked beside me

The winter storms made way for spring

In every season

From where I'm standing

I see the evidence of Your goodness

All over my life, all over my life

I see Your promises in fulfillment

All over my life, all over my life

Help me remember when I'm weak

Fear may come but fear will leave

Fill up to Spill out

You lead my heart to victory

And You always will be

I see the evidence of Your goodness

All over my life, all over my life

I see Your promises in fulfillment

All over my life, all over my life

I started this book searching for all the answers on how to be the best version of myself and how to live my very best life, and 2020 gave me those answers, loud and clear. The best version of myself and living my best life looks like finding the good in every season, even the really tough ones. It's about embracing who God made me to be and who I am becoming as I live to honor Him. It's about discovering what I need to pour into myself each day in order to create an overflowing cup of love, wisdom, and generous gifts to spill out to others. Living the dream is when life isn't just about me but loving and serving others with kindness and grace.

2020 has been hard, but it has also taught me so much, and I hope that in reading this book and going along this journey with me as I processed this year in real time, you feel encouraged to keep showing up, creating peace, joy, and purpose in your own beautiful life, even in the midst of a challenging season.

Covid-19 is nowhere close to being over with. As we approach the end of the year the numbers are sadly on the rise again. Over 250,000 people in our country have sadly lost their lives to this new virus and unfortunately many more will die as it spreads. We are still wearing masks and taking appropriate precautions, but definitely growing weary as each month passes. Fortunately, most kids are back at school (for now), people are working, church doors are open, and some familiar activities have returned, but everything still looks much different. As we wait for a vaccine, wait for unity and rebuilding of our country and what is good, we must choose to keep going, focusing on what truly matters, our faith, our family, and our purpose.

As I conclude this book, I encourage you to take time to thoughtfully evaluate what's important in your life, making time to intentionally fill your cup with those things each day, especially during your busiest and hardest seasons. We can't pour from an empty cup. We can't keep showing up well for others when we aren't taking time for ourselves. Make time for the things that matter. Focus on protecting your peace, cultivating joy, and doing the things that fill you up so you can keep spilling out to others. I'm praying for you, and I am praying for the healing of our land.

Acknowledgements

First and foremost, I have to thank my Creator and Savior for putting this book on my heart in a year that would challenge my faith in many ways. Thank you for revealing your goodness all over my life again and again, even in the middle of a tough year. It is possible to see the good when we are in constant pursuit of it.

Thank you to my husband Ted, for always supporting my investment in personal growth and allowing me time to fill my cup with the things that bring me peace and joy. Thank you for inspiring me to live a life of courage and purpose. I love you, and I love the life we have built together. Let us always be a couple that finishes what we've started.

Big buckets of gratitude to my daughters Avery and Natalie. You girls fill me up like nothing else. You bring me joy and happiness, give my life beautiful meaning and purpose, and you just make life more fun. I love being your Mom. I am incredibly blessed to have two beautiful daughters, and I love you both so much.

Thank you to my parents for showing me the importance of faith, family, and hard work. My childhood shaped me into the person I am today, and I am grateful for your endless love and beautiful example to our family.

To my tribe of friends, my LTD beach trip crew, my girls, thank you for being my community for all these years. Life is hard, but so much better with friends. I love our friendship and what it brings to my life, and I'm so glad we get to do life together.

Allison R. Smith

About the Author

Allison R. Smith is an author, writer, family nurse practitioner, wife to her college sweetheart Ted, and mother to two amazing girls, Avery and Natalie. She resides in Texas with her family and their incredibly spoiled Goldendoodle, Bella, along with a hamster named Patches and some fish. She enjoys running, reading and writing, photographing nature, traveling with her adventurous family, and encouraging others to cultivate peace, joy, and purpose in their lives. She feels passionate about the idea of filling your cup to spill out to others as the very best version of yourself.

Made in the USA
Coppell, TX
04 December 2020